KENDO

KENDO

Jeff Broderick

NEW HOLLAND

First published in 2004 by New Holland Publishers
London · Cape Town · Sydney · Auckland
www.newhollandpublishers.com

86 Edgware Road
London, W2 2EA
United Kingdom

80 McKenzie Street
Cape Town 8001
South Africa

14 Aquatic Drive
Frenchs Forest, NSW 2086
Australia

218 Lake Road
Northcote, Auckland
New Zealand

ISBN 1 84330 590 9 (paperback)

Publishing managers: Claudia dos Santos, Simon Pooley
Commissioning editor: Alfred LeMaitre
Publisher: Mariëlle Renssen
Studio manager: Richard MacArthur
Designer: Nathalie Scott
Design assistant: Jeannette Streicher
Editor: Anna Tanneberger
Picture Researcher: Karla Kik
Proofreader/Indexer: Leizel Brown
Production: Myrna Collins

Consultant: Paul Budden (6th Dan Renshi)

Reproduction by Unifoto, Cape Town
Printed and bound in Malaysia by Times Offset (M) Sdn. Bhd.

2 4 6 8 10 9 7 5 3 1

DISCLAIMER

The author and publishers have made every effort to ensure that the information contained in this book was accurate at the time of going to press, and accept no responsibility for any injury or inconvenience sustained by any person using this book or following the advice provided herein.

AUTHOR'S ACKNOWLEDGEMENTS

I would like to thank the following individuals without whom this book could never have been realized: The staff of New Holland Publishing for this opportunity, and particularly Anna Tanneberger and Alfred LeMaitre for their enthusiastic support; Fred Hunsberger, for his excellent photographs and his unflagging professionalism; Rob Beaton and Mike Zambakkides for technical support; and to Michael Castellani, Edward Chart, MiSoo Ko, Tyler Rothmar and Kim Taylor for modelling, for valuable input and, most importantly, for their friendship. To all my teachers in Canada and abroad: thank you for showing me The Way.

CONTENTS

I NTRODUCTION

Figures dressed in armour and dark, flowing clothing square off against one another. Wielding long, straight bamboo swords, their voices rise in high-pitched screams as they shift about, looking for an opening in their opponent's stance. The tips of their swords cross as they probe for any potential weakness. Sunlight glints off their metal facemasks and highly polished chest protectors. Suddenly, both lunge forward in a blur; the hall echoes with the thunderous sound of stamping feet, and the crack of bamboo across the chest protector. For many people, this is their first impression of the fascinating art known as kendo.

What is kendo?

Kendo is the art of Japanese fencing. The term literally means 'the way of the sword'. Students wear traditional clothing and protective armour, and wield a bamboo *shinai* — a safer replica of the Japanese *katana* sword. Practitioners, called *kendoka*, compete by attempting to strike an opponent's vital targets: the head, throat, wrists and abdomen. In tournaments three referees determine whether the strikes are valid, having been made with the correct technique: sword and body acting in concert. In addition to competitive play, kendo includes long hours spent perfecting basic techniques, and paired *kata* — a choreographed bout with a partner that teaches a specific method of attack and defence, emphasizing precision and correct form.

Why practise kendo?

Kendo is an exciting, invigorating activity that offers participants the opportunity to compete with others in a martial art that has been practised for hundreds of years. It is an art that places a strong emphasis on the unification of mind, body and spirit. Kendo will build physical endurance, sharpen reflexes, increase speed and build strength. Equally important, however, are its mental benefits. It is felt that a student's concentration, determination, competitive spirit, attitude, and character are also developed through continued practice.

Kendo is enjoyed by people of all ages, from very young children to senior citizens. Even people in their 80s and 90s continue to participate. Because kendo consists of more than just its sportive aspects, it is felt that mastering the art is a lifelong pursuit, and that training is never finished.

Kendo is an ancient martial art with roots in the sword training of the samurai in feudal Japan over 500 years ago. Thus, kendoka are not only playing a sport; they are also keeping alive a cultural tradition.

The reasons for practising Kendo are perhaps best summarized in an official statement from the All-Japan Kendo Federation, released in 1975:

The purpose of practising kendo is
- to mould the mind and body
- to cultivate a vigorous spirit.

And through correct and rigid training
- to strive for improvement in the art of kendo
- to hold in esteem human courtesy and honour
- to associate with others with sincerity, and
- to forever pursue the cultivation of oneself.

This will enable one to
- hold in esteem human courtesy and honour
- love his/her country and society
- contribute to the development of culture
- promote peace and prosperity among all peoples.

Kendo around the world

Kendo began in Japan, and continues to have its greatest following there. With over two million active

opposite DRESSED IN TRADITIONALLY STYLED ARMOUR, TWO KENDOKA FACE OFF, STANDING IN CHUDAN NO KAMAE.

kendoka, it is one of the most popular martial arts in Japan. Unfortunately, kendo is not yet as popular as other martial arts in some Western countries, so in many places it may be difficult to find a qualified kendo instructor. A list of national and international contacts is provided at the end of this book. Most kendoka belong to a national organization that is affiliated to the International Kendo Federation — a governing body that regulates kendo worldwide.

The IKF

The fact that there is only one organization means that kendo is practised in a very uniform, standardized way around the world. Players from one country can compete on an even playing field with players from any other country. The IKF works very closely with its most influential member association, the All-Japan Kendo Federation, to set guidelines and standards of competition and judging. In addition, the IKF is responsible for overseeing the World Kendo Championships, held every three years.

Grading in kendo

There are no coloured belts in kendo; the system is one of *kyu* grades and *dan* grades.

The hierarchy of ranks in ascending order		
Sankyu	Third *kyu*	
Nikyu	Second *kyu*	
Ikkyu	First *kyu*	
Shodan	First dan	
Nidan	Second dan	
Sandan	Third dan	
Yondan	Fourth dan	
Godan	Fifth dan	
Rokudan	Sixth dan	(*Renshi* — 'instructor')
Nanadan	Seventh dan	(*Kyoshi* — 'teacher')
Hachidan	Eighth dan	(*Hanshi* — 'master')

Ranks below *ikkyu* may not be officially recognized by some kendo associations. They are the responsibility of local clubs, and are given out to beginners upon the authority of the presiding *sensei*. From *ikkyu* and above, ranks are awarded on the basis of official examinations sponsored by the national kendo federation. On reaching the grade of *rokudan*, a kendoka is expected to become an instructor, and may be granted the title of *renshi*; the title implies a 'journeyman instructor' who has achieved a high level of skill, but who is still learning. Kendo instructors of seventh *dan* or higher may be given the title *kyoshi* or teacher. The highest possible rank in kendo is *hachidan hanshi*: this title implies a person who is a model for others to emulate, and is granted to those who have achieved near-complete mastery of kendo. In the past, kendo rankings went as high as ninth dan (*kyudan*), and tenth dan (*judan*), before the system was changed to the one in place today. There are a number of surviving ninth dan *sensei* in Japan today, but the highest grade currently awarded is *hachidan*.

The IKF also sets guidelines for grading require-ments, although some details and implementation vary from country to country. The chart on this page serves as a rough outline of the requirements for each grade.

The minimum time in which you can achieve eighth dan is 32 years, assuming every grading is passed on the first try. Each year, hundreds of seventh dan *sensei* gather in Kyoto and Tokyo for the test to be admitted into the ranks of *hachidan*; very few will succeed.

Kendo and other martial arts

The All-Japan Kendo Federation's main area of respon-sibility is, of course, kendo. It also oversees two other sword-related martial arts: iaido and jodo. Iaido is the art of drawing the *katana* from the scabbard, perform-ing a series of cuts, and then resheathing the blade. The Kendo Federation has a set of 12 techniques that are meant to teach the fundamentals of iaido to kendo practitioners, including how to handle a real sword.

Grade challenged	Minimum practice time since last grade	Minimum age
1 *(Ik)kyu*	– – –	– – –
1 *(Sho)dan*	Over 3 months after granting of 1 kyu	14 years and over
2 *(Ni)dan*	Over 2 years after granting of 1st dan	16 years and over
3 *(San)dan*	Over 2 years after granting of 2nd dan	18 years and over
4 *(Yon)dan*	Over 3 years after granting of 3rd dan	21 years and over
5 *(Go)dan*	Over 4 years after granting of 4th dan	25 years and over
6 *(Roku)dan*	Over 5 years after granting of 5th dan	30 years and over
7 *(Nana)dan*	Over 6 years after granting of 6th dan	36 years and over
8 *(Hachi)dan*	Over 10 years after granting of 7th dan	48 years and over

Jodo is the art of using a 1.2m (4ft) wooden staff to defeat an opponent armed with a sword. There are also 12 representative jodo techniques in the Kendo Fed-eration curriculum. Jodo teaches the importance of posture, distance, timing, and the correct application of strength. Not everyone who practises kendo prac-tises iaido or jodo, and vice versa. It is felt, however, that they are complementary arts, and that cross training can be valuable and enlightening; many high-ranking *sensei* hold ranks in multiple sword arts.

left JODO IS THE ART OF USING A 1.2M (4FT) WOODEN STAFF TO DEFEAT A SWORDSMAN, USING A SERIES OF BLOCKS, STRIKES, THROWS AND LOCKS.
opposite IAIDO IS ABOUT POWER AND PRECISION: DRAWING, EXECUTING A SERIES OF CUTS AND RESHEATHING THE SWORD.

AN EARLY PHOTOGRAPH SHOWING A WARRIOR IN FULL ARMOUR AND HELMET, WIELDING A KATANA.

History of swordsmanship in Japan

The *bushi*

The history of Japan is replete with unrest and almost constant civil war. The *bushi*, or warrior class, achieved power and social prominence in these turbulent times, as did their European counterparts, the knights. The *bushi* devoted a great deal of time and energy to honing their martial prowess, and the typical warrior's education encompassed many different skills including swordsmanship, archery, horseback riding, spear, polearm, grappling, and military strategy, among others. Schools arose that specialized in one or more areas of martial training, and eventually codified their teachings. At one time there were many of these schools, or *ryuha*, and some of them have survived hundreds of years in an unbroken lineage to the present day.

Kenjutsu

Kenjutsu is the art of the sword. Although it was never the most important weapon on the battlefield (that role belonged at various times to the bow, the spear and, eventually, the gun), the sword held a special place in the heart of the warrior. It was his own personal weapon, and last line of defence. It would be used in close combat should his other weapons fail. Furthermore, the sword had traditionally been assigned a divine aura, and swordsmanship was highly regarded by the warrior class. Eventually, as peace settled over Japan in the 17th century, attention shifted away from the battlefield weapons and to the use of the *katana*, the badge of the samurai class. Proficiency in the sword was seen as a desirable quality in a well-rounded samurai gentleman. Hundreds of *kenjutsu ryuha* were developed in this period, some of which are still practised to this day. *Kenjutsu* was typically learned using the *bokuto*, or wooden sword of roughly the same size and weight as a real *katana*. Although less lethal than its steel counterpart, a blow from a *bokuto* could still maim or even kill an opponent. Thus, practice was done as *kata*, or set-form practice sessions with a partner where the participants stopped their blows just before hitting the target. It would have been extremely dangerous to allow free sparring with a solid wooden sword. These *kata* taught correct handling of the sword, and fundamental principles of swordsmanship. In addition, many *kata* dealt with specific situations that might be encountered by a swordsman.

A WOODBLOCK PRINT SHOWING THREE SAMURAI, ONE ARMED WITH A SPEAR, ATTEMPTING TO SUBDUE AN ENEMY.

The sword and the spirit

After the battle at Sekigahara in 1600, when Tokugawa Ieyasu took military control of Japan, peace settled over the previously turbulent country. Within a century, battlefield arts were losing their relevance. Swordsmanship, however, retained much of its popularity because of its growing link with Zen Buddhism.

Freed from the pragmatic demands of near-constant war, and looking for ways to perfect their skills, swordsmen began to examine their art through the lens of philosophy. What mental state was best for the swordsman to achieve victory? Could an appreciation of Zen give a deeper insight to a swordsman? These sorts of questions were addressed in a number of Zen-related works on swordsmanship. Some of the most influential were written by the Rinzai Zen monk, Takuan Soho, who was the spiritual adviser to an emperor and two shogun. He was also friends with prominent swordsmen: Yagyu Munenori, master of the Yagyu Shinkage style of swordsmanship; Ono Tadaaki, founder of the Ono branch of the Itto style; and, purportedly, with Miyamoto Musashi, one of Japan's most famous swordsmen. In various works addressed to swordsmen, such as *The Mysterious Record of Immovable Wisdom* Takuan discusses the correct state of mind for a swordsman, and the concept of self and other. His works state that, in order to be successful, the swordsman must transcend mere physical technique and become the master of his mind as well.

Yagyu Munenori and Miyamoto Musashi both wrote scrolls on the topic of swordsmanship. Yagyu wrote the *Hereditary Book of Strategy*, or *Heiho Kaden Sho*, while Musashi's wisdom is recorded in the famous *Go Rin no Sho*, commonly known in the West as *The Book of Five Rings*. These scrolls are highly technical manuals on swordsmanship, but are infused with the sort of spiritual advice that Takuan gave to them.

Kendo today continues to place a strong emphasis on the link between technique and one's mental or spiritual state. This is quite succinctly stated in the following kendo meditation used in many *dojo*s in Japan. Note that the word for 'mind' might just as well be translated as 'heart'.

The Sword is the Mind.
When the Mind is right, the Sword will be right.
When the Mind is wrong, the Sword will also be wrong.
Those who wish to study kendo
Must first study the Mind.

The development of *bogu* and *shinai*

Some *sensei*, evidently dissatisfied with the limitations of *kata* practice, wanted to introduce an element of safe sparring to their practice sessions. In an effort to reduce some of the inherent dangers of *bokuto* practice, some *ryuha* implemented the use of protective gear. This took the form of large padded gloves and, occasionally, padded headgear. Using a more flexible weapon also reduced injuries. Instead of a solid wooden sword, some schools used a piece of bamboo, split many times and fully encased in leather. Eventually, this developed into a *shinai* similar to that seen in kendo today: four slats of bamboo held together in a leather sleeve.

One school that was instrumental in the development of protective equipment for swordsmen was the *Itto ryu* and its various branches. Originally founded by Kagehisa Ittosai Ito, considered one of the strongest swordsmen of the late Muromachi period, the *Itto ryu* was respected and influential. It is a student of the *Itto ryu*, Chuta Nakanishi, who is usually credited with the invention of the *kote* and four-slat *shinai*, circa 1770, still in use today.

Armour also gradually developed in the 18th and 19th centuries. The padded fabric or leather gloves (*kote*) and bamboo-ribbed chest protector (*do*) were followed by the *tare*, a protective skirt for the waist, and a revised helmet (*men*) with a metal grille to protect the face and eyes. By the 19th century, there were hundreds of schools using *shinai* and armour similar to that still in use today. The development of the *shinai* and protective equipment (*bogu*) gave a new, safer, competitive dimension to the art of swordsmanship and made the art very popular.

Kendo's emergence

Kendo grew in popularity and came to be appreciated as an excellent method of cultivating desirable characteristics in young people. In 1871 the government of Japan made kendo instruction mandatory in public schools. Young children began practising kendo in great numbers. The All-Japan Kendo Federation (Zen Nihon Kendo Renmei, or ZNKR) was formed in 1928 to oversee kendo training and to standardize its rules, equipment, *dojo*s, and teaching methods. The ZNKR also organized many public exhibitions of kendo and the first All-Japan kendo championships.

Brief decline

There was a brief period of decline, however, when Japan wholeheartedly embraced Western culture after years of self-imposed exile and extreme conservatism. Some people saw kendo as a relic of an undesirable past and membership declined as more and more students engaged in Western pursuits. It seemed that kendo might be headed for extinction. This trend was reversed, however, in the years leading up to World War II, when anti-Western sentiment was on the rise and interest in traditional cultural pursuits revived.

Japanese *budo*, as a representation of the country's unique warrior spirit, was embraced by nationalistic organizations using it to drum up support for Japan's aggressively expansionist policies. Due in part to this association, the practice of martial arts, including kendo, was banned by the occupation forces following Japan's surrender in 1945.

Postwar

Many kendoka continued to practise in secret for years until the ban was lifted. In October 1952, the ZNKR was re-established. Kendo was reformulated with new rules that forbade some of the more aggressive prewar practices such as throws and chokes.

Meanwhile, kendo began to grow in popularity in other countries, particularly those with large Japanese immigrant populations such as Brazil, the United States and Canada. In the 1950s and 1960s numerous international goodwill tournaments and seminars were held. The International Kendo Federation was founded in 1970, and the first World Kendo Championship tournament was held in Japan.

Kendo today

Kendo continues to grow in popularity on the international scene. Kendo world championships are held every three years, and each one features a greater number of participating nations. Currently, there are over 40 countries with national organizations belonging to the IKF. Millions of people are discovering this ancient discipline.

KENDO IS CONSIDERED AN EXCELLENT WAY OF CULTIVATING DESIRABLE CHARACTERISTICS IN YOUNG PEOPLE.

KENDO EQUIPMENT

The *shinai* consists of four pieces of bamboo, held together with a leather sleeve at the handle, a band near the tip, and a cap. The four bamboo slats are slightly flexible, making the *shinai* much less dangerous than a solid wood or steel weapon. Originally, there were no set regulations governing the size of the *shinai*. Consequently, some kendoka became famous for their use of extremely long *shinai* — some reached lengths of over 2m (6ft)! Eventually, the dimensions of the *shinai* were limited to about 1m (39in) or less. Today, some people (notably children and lighter women) choose to wield a shorter *shinai*.

Innovation to the centuries-old bamboo *shinai* includes a Japanese manufactured one using carbon fibre staves. They are more durable and require almost no maintenance, while similar in weight and feel to bamboo. They are, however, more expensive.

A string (*tsuru*) connects the tip (*sakigawa*), the *nakayui* (the leather wound around the forward third) and leather handle. This string serves another important function: it represents the back of the sword, so the opposite side is the cutting edge. All strikes in kendo must be performed as if your sword had a real edge. Strikes that smack the target with the sides of the *shinai* will not be counted.

On a real *katana* (*see p18*) only the forward third of the blade (*monouchi*) was used for cutting. The same applies in kendo. The *nakayui* holds the staves together and provides a demarcation line for the *monouchi*. Strikes below the *nakayui* are not counted. Striking the *tsuba* (round hand guard, made of hard leather or plastic) does not count either. The section from the *nakayui* forward, which must be used for striking, is called the *datotsu-bu*.

The *bokuto*

Sometimes called a *bokken*, the *bokuto* is made of solid wood. It is designed to have the weight, feel and balance of the real weapon, *katana,* or as close as possible. It is usually crafted out of oak, chosen for its strength and durability. In kendo, the *bokuto* is used to practise *kendo no kata*, the paired session of the All-Japan Kendo Federation. Both a long sword and a short sword are used, depending on the technique.

A CARBON (UPPER) AND BAMBOO (LOWER) *SHINAI*

B DISASSEMBLED *SHINAI*

C LONG AND SHORT *BOKUTO*

opposite THE LONG AND SHORT SWORDS WERE WORN PROUDLY BY THE SAMURAI AS THE BADGE OF THEIR CLASS. A PAIR SUCH AS THIS IS CALLED A *DAISHO*.

The *katana*

Although infrequently used by kendo practitioners, the *katana* is the original steel sword that was used in kendo techniques, and kendoka should have a thorough understanding of its parts and nomenclature.

The steel is tempered to give it a spine which is tough and flexible, and able to absorb impact without breaking. This steel core is jacketed in an extremely hard outer layer which, although fairly brittle, can be honed to a sharp edge. The razor sharpness of the sword has elevated it to near-mythical status. The scholarly study of Japanese swords, or *Nihon-to*, is a discipline unto itself, and can occupy a lifetime of research.

Shinai maintenance

Regular inspection of equipment is the duty of every kendo player. *Shinai* in particular must be carefully maintained to avoid, or detect, the formation of splinters, which can enter the grille and cause serious injury or blindness. Before use, a new *shinai* should be disassembled and the inner surfaces checked for splinters and sanded. The bamboo staves can then be soaked in a light oil.

Inspect your *shinai* for splinters before and after each practice. If you find a splinter, do not use that *shinai* until you have had a chance to disassemble it, remove the splinter, and apply oil if required.

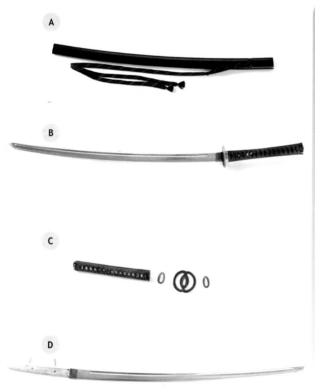

A THE SCABBARD (*SAYA*) AND CORD (*SAGEO*)

B THE *KATANA*

C THE HANDLE (*TSUKA*), SPACERS (*SEPPA*) AND GUARD (*TSUBA*)

D THE STRIPPED BLADE AND TWO RETAINING PEGS (*MEKUGI*)

Suggested *shinai* care

A new *shinai* is not ready for use upon purchase. First, it has probably been shipped with a number of protective strings binding the staves together; these should be cut off and discarded. Remove the hand guard and the rubber stopper, and examine the knot which ties the *tsuru* (string) to the leather *tsuka*, so that you get a sense of how it is tied. Undo this knot, and slide off the handle, and the entire string-*nakayui*-tip piece. Use a pencil to label the staves so that you know in what order to reassemble them — they will fit more perfectly if reassembled in order. Next, remove the rubber tip piece, and gently pry apart the staves. They are held together with a small square of metal near the bottom end.

Examine the staves carefully for splinters. Lightly sand the edges with a sanding block so that the contact surfaces are smooth. A new *shinai* should then be soaked in oil for a day or two, to prevent it from becoming too dry or brittle. A piece of pipe, slightly larger than a *shinai*, is useful for this purpose. Fill it with a light oil such as mineral oil, or oil designed for wood furniture, and immerse the staves. Do not soak the staves for more than a couple of days, as they can become oversaturated and heavy. Wipe off the excess oil, and reassemble the *shinai*.

Clothing and how to wear it (*hakama* and *keikogi*)

The kendo uniform (collectively called the *dogi*) consists of a jacket (the *uwagi* or *keikogi*) and a pleated, split skirt called the *hakama*. The jacket is usually closely stitched and quilted, which lends a degree of protection to the unarmoured parts of the body in the case of stray blows from the *shinai*. The *hakama* is belted tightly about the hips, but has roomy legs to allow for free movement.

Kendo clothing is traditionally dyed a deep blue colour using natural indigo. This dye is said to have an antibiotic effect, which tends to prevent the growth of bacteria and mould in hot, humid conditions. Black *hakama* are also commonly seen. The entire uniform can also be white. The *hakama* has seven pleats: five in front and two at the back. These pleats have been assigned a symbolic meaning, with each pleat standing for a particular samurai virtue:

Jin: goodwill, benevolence
Gi: honour, justice
Rei: courtesy, manners
Chi: wisdom, intelligence
Shin: truth, sincerity
Chu: loyalty
Ko: devoutness

The jacket is worn first, and often has inner and outer ties to keep it neatly closed (A). The *hakama* is worn next, with the upper hem tied just over the hips (B). It is then tied at the back (C), tied in front and the ends tucked in (D). Outward appearance is considered to be a reflection of character and inner state, so it is important to dress neatly and carefully. The jacket should not be allowed to fall open. No undershirt should be visible under the jacket. The length of the jacket must be such that no skin is visible between the bottom hem and the side slits of the *hakama*. The *hakama* should come to the ankle bone in length. Its backplate should be snug against the lower back, and the *hakama* should be tied on the hips so that there is a slight angle on the lower hem: the back of the *hakama* should be slightly higher than the front. All rips and tears should be patched, and there should be no loose or dangling straps.

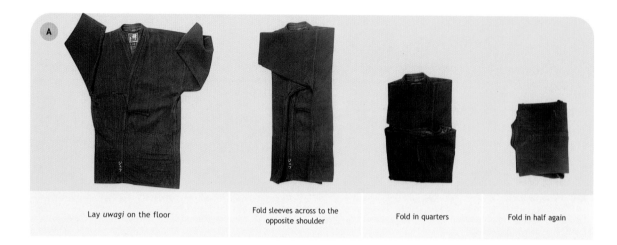

A

Lay *uwagi* on the floor

Fold sleeves across to the opposite shoulder

Fold in quarters

Fold in half again

Keep your uniform in good shape by folding it properly after every practice. *Hakama* will lose their pleats if they are not cared for. To wash your uniform, be aware that some kendo clothing is dyed with non-colourfast indigo dye. Always wash your clothing by hand, separately, and in cold water. New uniforms can have the dye 'set' by soaking in a mixture of cold water and rice vinegar. Hang to dry, out of direct sunlight, and once dry, fold immediately to preserve the pleats.

A FOLDING THE *UWAGI*

B FOLDING THE *HAKAMA*

C TYING THE STRAPS

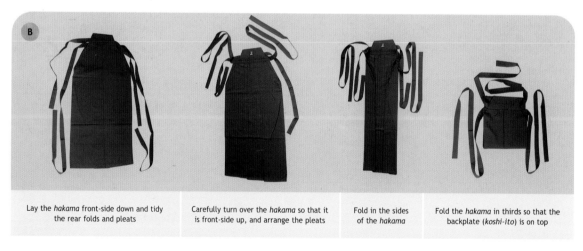

B

Lay the *hakama* front-side down and tidy the rear folds and pleats

Carefully turn over the *hakama* so that it is front-side up, and arrange the pleats

Fold in the sides of the *hakama*

Fold the *hakama* in thirds so that the backplate (*koshi-ito*) is on top

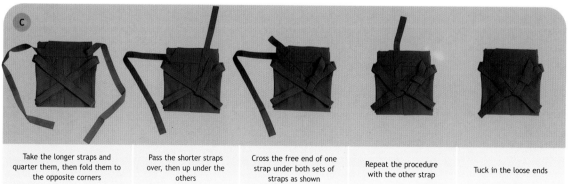

C

Take the longer straps and quarter them, then fold them to the opposite corners

Pass the shorter straps over, then up under the others

Cross the free end of one strap under both sets of straps as shown

Repeat the procedure with the other strap

Tuck in the loose ends

The *bogu*

The protective equipment is referred to collectively as the *bogu*. It consists of the *men*, or helmet; the *do*, or breastplate; the *kote*, or gloves; and the *tare*, a sectioned apron that protects the groin. The *do* is made of many thin bamboo strips (or in some inexpensive modern versions, a formed fibreglass shell) covered in lacquered hide. The other components are generally made of thick quilted cotton, with stitching and leather reinforcements. They are designed to absorb and redistribute the shock of a blow rather than deflect the impact.

Beginners will not wear the armour immediately. Instead, their first lessons will focus on the basics of correct footwork, body movement, and sword handling. This preliminary stage usually lasts a few months, or until the *sensei* feels the student is ready to progress to wearing armour. Although many students are anxious to begin wearing armour right away and to commence full-contact sparring, it is important to concentrate on developing strong basic techniques first.

When the time comes to don the armour, the club may have sets available for use by beginners. They may ask for a deposit or rental fee. This is a good investment because buying *bogu* can be very expensive, and you will want to be sure that kendo is right for you before you make the monetary commitment to buying your own set. Eventually, however, you will want to purchase a set of your own.

Buying *bogu*

Until quite recently, buying *bogu* outside Japan was rather challenging. Fortunately, there are now many companies that export *bogu* around the world. The first decision to be made is how much to spend. A starter set, suitable for a beginner, can be found at an affordable price, but there is almost no upper limit to how much you can spend. Cheaper sets tend to be machine manufactured, while more expensive sets are partially or entirely handmade. At one time, there was a large gap in quality between machine-made and handmade *bogu*. However, these days the difference in quality is hardly noticeable.

Another rating of quality is in terms of the stitching size. The entire fabric surface of *bogu* is covered in small stitches that serve as quilting, helping to give the

A THE *MEN*, OR HELMET

B THE *DO*, OR BREASTPLATE

C THE *KOTE*, OR GLOVES

D THE *TARE*, A SECTIONED APRON THAT PROTECTS THE GROIN

armour its stiffness. In general, the closer together the stitching, the more rigid and durable the *bogu* will be. Thus, a smaller stitch size is desirable in most cases. A beginner's *bogu* set might have a stitching size of 6mm (¼in) or more, while an expensive set could have a stitch size close to 2mm (¹⁄₁₆in). Next, the structure of the *do* is variable: cheaper sets will have *do* made of fibreglass; more expensive *do*s are made of genuine bamboo staves. The more staves, the more expensive the *do* tends to be. The covering of the *do* can also be very fancy and colourful, with elaborate embroidery and exotic materials such as sharkskin, costing more money. Finally, the metal grille on the *men* is made of

different materials. In an expensive set, the grille is titanium or of other lightweight alloys; on cheaper sets, it is heavier steel.

The most important factor when buying *bogu* is to ensure a good fit. The chin and the forehead must fit snugly into the *men* padding without being too tight, and the *monomi* (the slightly wider gap in the grille) should be directly in front of the eyes. The *kote* should be comfortable, and the *do* roomy, with space between it and the body so that impacts are not transmitted to the sides of the body. A reputable *bogu* dealer should ask for your full body measurements before selling you anything.

LIKE SAMURAI ARMOUR OF OLD, TOP QUALITY KENDO ARMOUR IS PAINSTAKINGLY HAND-CRAFTED BY SKILLED ARTISANS. ADVANCES IN TECHNOLOGY HAVE MEANT THAT MACHINE-MADE ARMOUR NOW APPROACHES THE QUALITY OF HAND-MADE ARTICLES.

Section: putting on *bogu*

1. The *tare* and all the components of the *bogu* should be put on while sitting properly in *seiza*, the formal seated position. Place the waistband part of the *tare* so that the bottom edge is even with the crease between the abdomen and top of the thighs (A). The point here is not to tie the *tare* too high on the body. Bring the ties around the body, keeping them flat at the back (B). Bring the ties around the body and tie them under the front flap, tucking up any loose ends (C).

2. The *do* is then placed against the chest (A). Take one of the upper cords, cross it behind your back, and bring it over the opposite shoulder. Pass it through the loop and tie it (B) — shown here while repeating the sequence on the other side. Next, tie the bottom cords behind you (C). These need not be particularly tight, but they should not be sloppy.

Thread the *himo* through the loop from behind. Pull the *himo* taut and hold the *do* in its final position.

Make a small loop with your thumb

Pass the free end of the *himo* behind the upper portion

Form a small loop out of the free end and pass about one inch of this loop through the first loop

Push down on the knot to tighten it against the *do*. If the remaining strings are long, tuck them neatly behind the *do* so that they do not get loose during practice

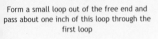

3. The *tenugui* or head towel is a rectangular cloth that is worn underneath the *men*. It absorbs sweat, keeps the hair out of the face, and provides an additional layer of padding on the head. The *tenugui* can be either folded around the head or can be folded first and then put on (*see illustration below*).

Hold the *tenugui* by the two bottom corners (A). Pull the rear edge of the *tenugui* back over your head (B). Maintaining tension in the cloth, bring the right corner to the left side of the head (C). Tightly pull the left corner of the *tenugui* to the right side of the head and tuck in this loose end to keep it in place (D). Fold the front portion of the *tenugui* up off the face (E). The ears may be tucked under the *tenugui*, or left out, according to personal preference.

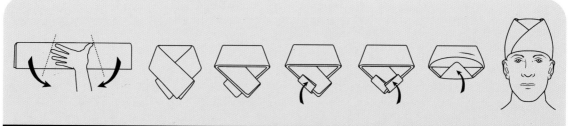

ALTERNATIVE METHOD OF PUTTING ON THE *TENUGUI*, BY FOLDING IT FIRST.

4. The *men* is perhaps the most difficult item for beginners to wear properly. First, arrange the cords in preparation. Then, holding the *men* by the grille, put it on your head, ensuring that your chin and forehead are snugly placed on the padding inside. Pull the cords forward to tighten the *men* (A). Cross them behind the head, and tie a bow knot (B). The cords should lie neatly in two lines along the side of the *men*, with no twists. Adjust the length of the remaining cords so that the loops and strings hang equally.

5. The *kote* should be put on last. Push your hand into the *kote* while holding the mitt with the opposite hand (C). This prevents strain on the stitching and will make your *kote* last longer. Place the left *kote* on first, then the right.

After practice, remove the right *kote* first by pulling from the tubular gauntlet, and then the left.

Putting on your *bogu* is something that takes getting used to. It is a good idea to practise putting this on at home until you get used to how it is done, and can dress quickly. That way, you don't keep other players waiting for you to get dressed.

After use, the *bogu* must be packed away neatly (D). Begin by folding up the loose straps of the *tare*. Place the *tare*, inside out, around the outside of the *do*. The *do* cords are then used to tie the *tare* to the *do*, making a package. Place the *men* and *kote* inside the *do*. If you have had a heavy practice session and your equipment is saturated with sweat, be sure to allow your *bogu* to air-dry naturally.

A TIGHTENING THE *MEN* CORDS

B REAR VIEW OF THE *MEN*, TIED

C PUTTING ON THE *KOTE*

D THE *BOGU* PACKED AWAY

PREPARATION

When entering the training hall, remove your footwear before stepping onto the practice surface. This serves the practical purpose of keeping the floor free of debris, but it also acknowledges the belief that the *dojo* is a sanctified area, worthy of our deepest respect. Bow to the front of the room before entering and on leaving. In some *dojo*s, this area will have a small shrine or perhaps a picture of an important teacher. In other *dojo*s, the end of the hall furthest from the entranceway serves as the focal point of the room. Bowing before entering and on leaving is a way of paying respect to fellow practitioners and to all the kendoka who have gone before.

Bear in mind that the procedures vary from place to place, so that when visiting an unfamiliar *dojo* for the first time, pay close attention to what the senior students are doing, and follow their example.

Opening etiquette and *mokuso* (meditation)

The usual etiquette is that students line up with the most senior at the far end of the room, and the most junior closest to the door. The senior student will call everyone to line up, and then to sit in *seiza*, the formal kneeling posture. Wait for the person on your left to sit before sitting down. The *shinai* is placed on

left AT THE COMMAND OF *'SEIRITSU!'* KENDO PLAYERS LINE UP AND STAND AT ATTENTION BEFORE PRACTICE BEGINS.

opposite WHEN SITTING IN *SEIZA*, THE FORMAL SEATED POSITION, YOU SHOULD MAINTAIN GOOD POSTURE BY KEEPING YOUR BACK STRAIGHT. PLACE YOUR HANDS NATURALLY, NEATLY BUT RELAXED, ON YOUR UPPER THIGHS. *SEIZA* IS ALSO THE POSITION IN WHICH KENDOKA MEDITATE.

the left side, with the *tsuba* in line with the knees and the string down. If the students are to be wearing armour, they will have already donned the *tare* and *do,* and will place the *kote* and *men* in front and to their right (A). The senior student (*sempai*) now calls '*Mokuso,*' the instruction to meditate.

Kendo has been influenced over the years by Zen meditation. *Mokuso* is essentially a short period of reflection or meditation. Place the hands in the lap with left palm up over the right, and gently touch thumbs as if you were cradling an egg. Keeping your back straight, and pulling in your chin, close your

eyelids halfway and focus on a spot on the floor approximately 2m (6ft) in front of you (B). Focus on your breathing cycle as you draw air in with the diaphragm. *Mokuso* is your opportunity to clear your mind of your daily troubles. Leave behind any aggression you may be feeling and mentally prepare yourself for the training to come.

Following *mokuso*, the senior student will direct you to turn to the focal point of the room, and bow. Then, perform a bow to the *sensei* who will be instructing you (C). Often, kendoka will say '*Onegaishimasu*' at this point, meaning 'If you please' or in the context of the *dojo*, 'Please teach me.' You are politely requesting instruction from your seniors.

Warming up and stretching

Following the opening, most *dojo*s will begin with a routine of stretching and warming up. The benefits of warming up and stretching are:

- the prevention of injury
- increased flexibility
- increased speed and power
- increased heart rate and blood flow
- settling the mind.

The following stretches are typical for kendo, and target those areas of the body which are most susceptible to injury: shoulders, groin and calves. The stretch routine will vary from place to place. You may find yourself at a *dojo* with a stretch routine that you feel is too brief, or you may for other reasons decide that you need extra time for stretches. In that case you can arrive at the *dojo* before the scheduled practice and spend as much time as you need doing your own stretches that target your personal problem areas. Then join in the standard group warm-up as directed by your *sensei*. In most *dojo*s, group warm-up is done in a large circle. The *shinai* are placed toward the centre of the circle when not in use.

A stretching routine

A good habit to adopt is to start at the top of the body and gradually work downward. When stretching, it is important to breathe, and to relax. Although it may be tempting to hold your breath while stretching, concentrate on breathing deeply and naturally. Stretching movements should be done slowly, and under control. Lunging into a stretch, or excessive 'bouncing' while stretching, can lead to injuries. As a guideline, the following actions should be performed eight times each.

⇦ **1) Neck**

A) With the arms and shoulders relaxed, dip the chin to touch the upper chest. Return to the natural position, then lift the chin toward the ceiling.

B) Next, look from side to side, rotating your head through the full natural range.

C) While facing forward, tilt the head from side to side. The feeling is that of placing your ear down onto your shoulder.

D) Finish with gentle circles in both directions. The feeling is of rolling the head around the shoulders and chest.

⇨ **2) Shoulder shrugs**

Keeping the arms relaxed and hanging at your sides, shrug the shoulders forward and backward in a circular motion.

⇦ **3) Arm circles**

Working with one arm at a time, swing the entire arm in a gentle, vertical circle, first forward and then backward. Once the shoulders and chest are loosened, do the same exercise with both arms swinging together, forward and backward.

⇨ **4) Shoulder stretches**

Hold your upper arm across your chest, cradling it in the elbow of your other arm and apply pressure toward your chest. This stretches the shoulder and triceps. Next, with your elbow up, and your hand and forearm hanging down behind your neck, grasp your elbow and push it back, stretching the triceps and shoulder. Repeat on the other side.

⇦ **5) Torso rotations**

Keeping the arms loose and allowing them to swing freely, rotate the upper body from side to side. The legs should be mostly stationary, and the rotation will twist the trunk and lower back.

⇦ **6) Bending**

Stand with the feet slightly wider than shoulder width apart. Placing the hands together, bend forward to touch the ground between your feet, then swing upward and back, bowing out the trunk and stretching the abdominal muscles.

⇨ **7) Hip circles**

Place the hands on the hips and try to make large, horizontal circles with the hips, in both directions. Keep the knees mostly locked so that the motion loosens the lower back and groin.

⇦ **8) Knee bends**

Place the hands on the knees. Go into a squat with the knees together, then rise up into a knees-locked position with the heels down.

⇨ **8) Knee circles**

Stand, feet together, bend your knees and cup them with your hands. Keeping your knees together, make circles over your feet by turning your knees to the left, then to the back (straightening your knees) and to the right (bending them) and forward. Repeat and change direction.

⇦ **9) Groin stretch**

Place the feet about twice shoulder width apart. Bend your right knee and lean deeply to that side, while keeping the left leg straight, the sole of that foot on the floor. Hold this position for a slow count of eight. Without straightening up, move your torso to the left side, straightening your right leg and bending your left leg as you do so. Again hold for a count of eight.

⇨ **10) Hamstring stretch**

With the feet about twice shoulder width apart, bend your left leg and lower your weight onto the ball of your left foot, with your right leg out straight to the side, resting on the heel. You should feel the stretch in the hamstring of the right leg. Repeat on the other side. Move into this position gently. Many people find it difficult to balance in this position, so support yourself with your hands on the floor if necessary.

⇩ **11) Calf stretch**

A) With the hips square to the front, step back with your right foot and bend the left (front) leg. Press the heel of your right foot (back) to the floor for a slow count of eight. Repeat on the other side.

B) Stand with your feet at their natural width, toes pointing forward. Move your left foot back. Bend the knees, lowering yourself, while keeping your heel flat on the floor, until you feel a stretch in the calf. Hold for a slow count of eight. Repeat on the other side.

⇦ **12) Wrists, fingers, ankles, toes**

This is often done individually. Roll the wrists and ankles to limber up the hands and feet. Gently bend the fingers with the opposite hand. Bend the toes back and forth by pressing them against the floor.

Floor exercises

The legs (particularly the groin, calf muscles and Achilles tendon) are the most likely to be injured in kendo. Some extra stretching may be appropriate, although it is not done at all *dojo*s.

A) Sit on the floor with your legs straight in front of you. Ensure that you are sitting forward, with a straight back and not on the flesh of your buttocks. Spread the legs as wide apart as possible. Gently lower your torso onto the front of your left leg and hold for a slow count of eight. Remember to breathe. Repeat on the other side.

B) Sit with your legs straight in front of you. Bend your left leg back so that the heel of your foot is up near the outside of your left hip. Lean back until you feel the stretch in the front of your left thigh, and hold for a slow count of eight. Repeat on the other side.

C) Sit with the soles of your feet touching. Grasp the ankles and pull the feet toward the groin. Press down on the knees gently with the elbows and stretch the groin, holding for a count of eight.

D) Sit with your legs straight in front of you. Sit forward, with straight back, and not on the flesh of your buttocks. Lengthen your spine upward before bending forward from the hips. Slowly take the front of your chest forward toward your feet. Take hold of your toes with your hands and gently pull yourself forward.

Warming up

Warming up the muscles and increasing blood flow is crucial to preventing injury. The following exercises should be done at a very gentle pace. The tempo can be slowly increased as the participants warm up.

E) Jumping

Begin with a slight bounce up and down, using the calf muscles and not the knees. Gradually increase the range of motion to a low hop, and eventually jump as high as you can, using the spring in your calves.

F) Swinging the *shinai*

Stand with the feet shoulder width apart and grip the *shinai* in both hands. The movement starts with the hands up and behind the head, the *shinai* straight down behind the back, the tip pointing at the floor and almost touching the buttocks. Concentrate on moving the *shinai* tip as the hands and arms swing forward in a large vertical circle and down to the point where the tip is almost hitting the floor in front. It is

perhaps ³/₄ of a vertical circle. One of the important points is that the tip travels straight up and straight down, not wobbling or wavering from side to side (as would happen if one were using too much of one hand or the other). Keep the back straight.

Note that this is NOT a strike, but a warm-up, and should be done with arms relaxed. Normally, one would start with the hands directly overhead, with the *shinai* itself no further back than horizontal to the floor, and finish by swinging straight forward to the target (be it the head, abdomen, or wrist). In this exercise, however, the range of motion is expanded.

MANY PROMINENT KENDO *SENSEI* RECOMMEND JOGGING DAILY, TO STRENGTHEN THE LEGS AND BUILD ENDURANCE. TREADMILLS AND STAIR CLIMBERS ARE ALSO USEFUL.

Strikes

The warm-up will almost certainly include a number of strikes with the *shinai*, performed individually. Strikes will be covered in the following sections. Concentrate on moving your body properly: large motions, no extraneous movements, and the tip of your *shinai* always moving up and down the centreline.

Further conditioning

You may find it beneficial to supplement your kendo practice with crosstraining. Many prominent kendo *sensei* recommend jogging daily, to strengthen the legs and build endurance. Machines such as stair climbers are also useful.

Since power in kendo comes not from the upper body but rather from the 'core' muscles, sit-ups and squats are recommended. Strong calves will help to make strikes more explosive and prevent injuries to the lower leg. Cycling is a good way to train the leg muscles. Finally, swimming is seen as a very good all-round exercise that trains the entire body while being gentle on joints.

BASIC TECHNIQUES

Regardless of whether you are right- or left-handed, the *shinai* is held in the same way. The left hand holds the *shinai* at the very bottom of the *tsuka*, the little finger flush with the end (A). The right hand holds it near the *tsuba* (B). The way in which you hold a sword is different to the way you hold any other object. The little finger grips with full strength, the next two fingers grip at about half-strength, and the index finger curls loosely around the sword with almost no strength. The *tsuka* should be pulled tightly into the heel of the hand. The V-shaped webbing between thumb and index finger is placed over the top of the *shinai* (C and D), so that the wrists feel rolled inward slightly and the thumbs feel as though they are pointing toward the floor. This grip frees the wrists and facilitates quick, sharp movements of the sword. Gripping too tightly and clenching the fists (like the grip on a baseball bat, for example) will only make the *shinai* stiff and lifeless, and must be avoided.

The elbows should have a natural curve. The heel of the left hand (and the end of the *tsuka*) should be a fist width in front of the *tanden*, which is about 4cm (2in) below the navel. Finally, avoid the temptation to tighten the shoulders.

When striking with the *shinai*, power is applied predominantly through the left hand, not the right. Many beginners use their right arm to power their strikes. However, the hand at the bottom end of the *shinai* (always the left) should provide the power, while the right hand is used to guide the *shinai*'s path.

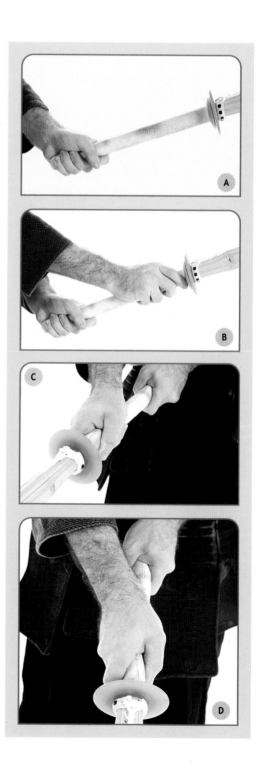

opposite *AI-UCHI* OCCURS WHEN TWO STRIKES LAND AT THE SAME INSTANT. HERE, THE KENDOKA ON THE RIGHT HAS STRUCK *DO* JUST AS THE KENDOKA ON THE LEFT IS STRIKING *MEN*.

Kamae (stance)

In the course of kendo's history, a large number of different stances and postures were developed within the various schools and traditions. Each stance was thought to have different strengths or tactical advantages that made it appropriate in different situations. In modern kendo, there are five main stances or *kamae*.

Chudan no kamae (the middle stance)

The first and most important stance in kendo is the middle stance, *chudan no kamae* (A). It is so fundamental to kendo that, if you are told to 'go into *kamae*', the reference is inevitably to *chudan no kamae*.

Chudan no kamae (or *chudan* for short) is perfectly balanced between defence and offence.

The left hand is one fist width in front of the *tanden* (B). The tip of the sword is pointed directly at the opponent's throat. The knee of the right leg

is bent very slightly while the left knee is straight but not locked. The left heel is raised about 2cm (1in) off the floor (C). The right foot is nearly flat on the floor, but the weight rests on the ball of the foot so that a single sheet of paper could be inserted between the heel and the floor. The feet are about one fist width apart, and the toes of the left foot are in line with the right heel. Both feet are pointed directly forward. It is sometimes said that the perfect foot position is found by walking in a natural manner, then stopping in mid-stride after having stepped forward with the right foot. This will leave the feet in a natural, correct position.

Unlike some martial arts that deal with the potential of multiple attackers or circular rotating motions, the stance in kendo is designed to direct all the power in a straight line forward at a single front-facing opponent. The heels must not be allowed to 'fall off line' so that the toes no longer point to the front. The hips should also be square to the front. Keep the legs springy (flexible and tensioned, in a state of readiness to push off), with the weight distributed about 60% on the front foot, 40% on the rear foot.

Kamae (stance or posture)

Chudan no kamae — middle level position
Jodan no kamae — high level position
Gedan no kamae — low level position

Other *kamae*

There are a number of other *kamae* which are seen in kendo, particularly in the *kendo no kata*.

■ *Jodan no kamae* (D) – 'high' level position in which the *shinai* is held above the head and ready to strike. This posture is very aggressive, but it leaves the body more open to attack. The left hand should be held directly above the forehead. There are actually two different *jodan* stances: right and left (*see p81*).

■ *Gedan no kamae* (E) – 'low' level position, with the *shinai* held down and in front of one's own right knee. This *kamae* exposes targets and invites attack, opening the opponent to a counterattack.

■ *Kamae o toku* – falling *kamae* or broken *kamae*; position of no advantage. It signifies the release of a stance. It is similar to *gedan* except that the sword is rolled slightly outward, signifying a subtle lowering of aggression.

Although these kendoka are shown wearing armour and handling a shinai, the positions being illustrated are specific to kata practice, when kendoka normally don't wear armour and use a bokuto instead of a shinai.

- *Hasso no kamae* (F) — a posture which strikes a balance between offence and defence. The sword is held high and ready to strike, while the elbows protect the *do*. The sword is held at a slight angle so that the *tsuba* is directly beside the mouth, the right hand next to the chin and the left hand in the centre of the chest. There is a natural tendency to lift the elbows upon adopting *hasso no kamae*. However, the shoulders and arms should be relaxed.

- *Waki gamae* (G) — the purpose of this stance is to hide the sword from the opponent's view. It is said to be especially useful when one's sword has snapped. Hiding the sword behind the body conceals the extent of the break, and makes it difficult for the opponent to judge the range of the remaining blade. The body is rotated, so that the opponent is viewed over the left shoulder. The hands hold the sword in direct contact with the right hip. The left hand grips normally, but the right hand must relax and open slightly in order to allow the sword to dip back and down behind the body.

Moving

Kendo has a particular manner of moving called *suri ashi* (sliding footwork). It's purpose is to preserve a strong posture, maintain balance, and ensure that movement is always possible in any direction.

The basic rule is that movements are always made with the leading foot. For example, moving forward is done by sliding the front foot forward, and quickly pulling up the rear foot to resume the correct stance. Moving backward, you should first move the back foot, then pull the front foot. Moving right, you start with the right foot; moving left, start with the left. Never cross your feet (unless using *ayumi ashi*), and always ensure that each step ends with the feet in the correct position. The left heel should be about one inch off the ground, ensure that the feet have not fallen off line but the toes are pointing directly forward, and the toes of the left foot are in line with the heel of the right. This method of walking, where the feet do not cross, is called *okuri ashi*, or a shuffle step. A normal walking step, where the feet cross, is called *ayumi ashi*.

When moving, do not step by raising the toes and placing the heel. Rather, slide the entire foot forward, maintaining contact with the floor. You will need to keep your front knee bent very slightly, so that it is springy. Take a fairly small step, so that you do not over-extend and lose your balance. To move more quickly, one needs to take faster small steps, rather than increase the length of each step.

It is said that movement in kendo is done from the hips. People tend to move with the head and upper body and lean in the direction they intend to go. This not only compromises balance, but tells your opponent what you are planning. In kendo, you should keep the upper body relaxed when moving. As a result your body moves as a single unit, without wavering or leaning from side to side.

Practise the following movement patterns until they become natural. Stay relaxed and check periodically to ensure that your feet are maintaining their correct placement. If you have a mirror,

observe yourself to make sure that your head is not bobbing up and down, but maintains a steady level as you move smoothly. Do these with and without a *shinai* in your hands. When holding the *shinai*, keep a strong *kamae* with your power directed forward, regardless of which way you are moving.

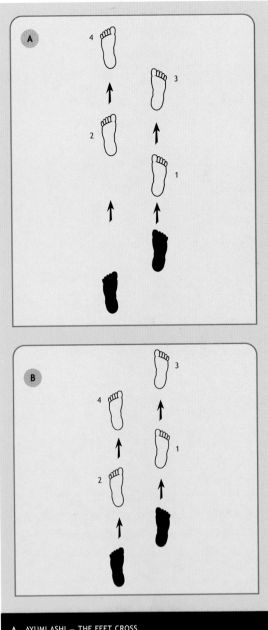

A AYUMI ASHI — THE FEET CROSS.

B OKURI ASHI — THE FEET NEVER CROSS.

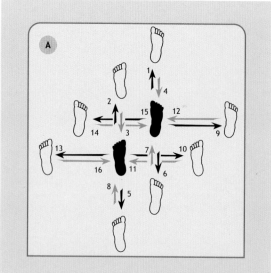

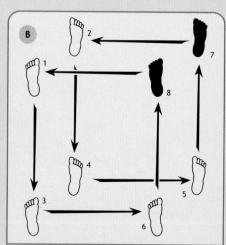

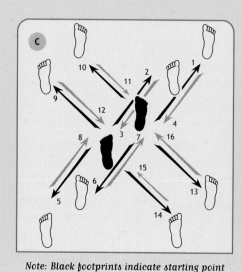

Note: Black footprints indicate starting point

A. The Cross

Move forward one step, then back; back again, then forward. Step right, then left; left again, then right. You have returned to your original position and you have traced out a cross shape.

B. The Box

Trace out a box by stepping forward, left, back, and right. Reverse the sequence so that you also move in a clockwise direction.

C. The 'X'

Similar to the cross, but try moving on diagonals to trace out an X-pattern on the floor.

Targets and strikes

There are four main targets in kendo:

- the head (*men*), which includes the centre of the head (*shomen*) and the upper corners of the head (*sayu-men*)
- the wrist (*kote*)
- the sides of the torso (*do*)
- the throat (*tsuki*).

When you strike a target, you must 'call' the attack by shouting the name of the target area. This is known as a '*kiai*' and is the vocal demonstration of your fighting spirit. The loud shouts (*kiai*) of kendo players during practice is one of the art's most distinctive features.

Before you begin practising these attacks against actual opponents, you will spend some time performing them individually. When practising these techniques, imagine that your opponent is the same height as you. Stop each strike at the correct position as if there were someone in front of you. As a general rule, raise the *shinai* directly over your head, with the tip leading the motion and tracing a line directly up the centre of your body. Do not pause at the top of the motion; rather, make one continuous motion. Use the left hand to power the *shinai*, not the right. If you are right-handed, you may have to concentrate on keeping the right hand relaxed.

⇨ **Men**

Begin in *chudan no kamae*. Raise the *shinai* straight up and over your head. Beginners have a tendency to make this motion too small, so be sure that the hands are directly over your head. Strike forward to your own forehead height with a loud shout of *'Men!'* Use the left hand to power the *shinai*. The feeling here should be that you are holding a broom, and trying to sweep cobwebs from the ceiling. Keep the hands relaxed until the point of 'impact' at which time you wring the wrists inward slightly and tighten your little fingers. The strike finishes with the arms straight out from the shoulders.

⇦ **Kote**

Similar to *men*, begin in *chudan no kamae*, and raise the *shinai* over your head. Strike down to the height of your own right wrist, and shout *'Kote!'* Keep the arms and hands relaxed until the point of 'impact', then tighten the grip and wring the hands inward. Finish with the *shinai* pressed forward and almost horizontal.

⇨ **Do**

Do has the same feeling as *men* and *kote*. Raise the *shinai* directly up the centreline and over your own head. Bring the *shinai* forward with the left hand, holding centre, while the right hand directs the tip of the *shinai* slightly out and to the left. Snap the *shinai* to the correct finishing spot, which is the opponent's right side. Shout *'Do!'* It is important to lead the strike with the correct angle, always imagining that the *shinai* has a cutting edge (opposite the *tsuru* string) and angling this edge into the target.

⇦ **Tsuki**

Tsuki is sometimes regarded as an advanced technique. It can be dangerous if improperly executed, and it is also considered improper to *tsuki* someone of higher rank than you in practice, so you should not use this technique unless you are given permission to do so.

Starting from *chudan*, thrust straight to the height of your own throat, using a forward sliding step, and a short but sharp thrust forward with the arms. Shout *'Tsuki!'* Do not bend forward at the waist; keep your back straight. *Tsuki* is made only to the small pad on the front of the *men*, which covers the throat.

Strikes with footwork

Men, *kote*, and *do* strikes can be practised with or without accompanying footwork. To do the strikes with footwork, follow this basic pattern:

- Begin in *chudan no kamae*.
- Raise the *shinai* directly overhead.
- Begin to strike down as the right foot slides forward.
- At the moment you finish the strike and wring the hands, *kiai* while sharply bringing the rear foot up to the correct position.

As this becomes more natural, the last two steps become combined into a single, continuous motion. Do not stop the *shinai* at the top of its path.

Strikes with stamping (*Fumikomu*)

The next exercise in striking is to attack with a strong leap forward. This is the characteristic stamping attack of kendo. To perform this strike:

1. Begin in *chudan no kamae* and apply pressure forward with the tip of the *shinai*.
2. Raise the *shinai* overhead, and continue to push forward with the body, keeping the back straight.
3. With a feeling of moving forward from the hips, strike forward with the *shinai*. Just as the balance begins to shift to the front, push strongly off the left foot, taking a large step forward with the right foot.
4. At the same instant the *shinai* hits the target, the right foot stomps powerfully down onto the floor, catching your balance. Make a loud *kiai*. The left foot immediately moves up to the right heel, re-establishing the proper stance.

After completing the strike, continue moving forward past the opponent, using *suri ashi* (*see p43*). Keep your hands at the same height as the finishing point of the strike. For example, if you strike *men*, keep the hands and arms extended at shoulder height.

Points to observe when doing *fumikomu*

- ■ This is not a jump forward. It has the feeling of launching forward with the hips and, at the last moment, catching the balance by stomping the right foot.
- ■ The left foot must not kick up off the ground.

- Do not allow the left heel to turn off line.
- The right foot should come down all at once — do not pound the heel into the floor.

An important concept in kendo is that of *'ki-ken-tai-ichi'* which literally means 'the spirit, sword, and body as one'. This concept is evident in this technique, since the *kiai*, strike, and the right-foot-stamp must occur at the same instant. In a tournament, a point will not be awarded unless these three elements combine simultaneously. You must pay close attention to your own timing as you practise.

Following through

Kendo attacks must be performed with a strong sense of commitment. It will not suffice to attempt an attack half-heartedly in the hope that it might succeed. Your attitude must be confident and determined. To show this sense of determination, after an attack is made you must let your forward momentum carry you past your opponent, using *suri ashi,* as you maintain a strong posture with the back straight and the arms extended. Moving past the opponent is done differently depending on which strike is being performed.

- Following a *men* strike, it is most common to move through on the right side. Keep the hands and arms extended at shoulder level and the *shinai* at head height.
- Following a *kote* strike, it is easiest to move past on the left side.
- You can move through a *do* strike in one of two ways. The most common is to strike *do* on the left, then allow the *shinai* to fold backward as you pass the opponent on the right. A second way to do this is to strike on the left, and simply move straight through on the left side.

Haya-suburi

Haya-suburi (fast practice swinging) is a technique used as a warm-up and conditioning exercise. Essentially, as the name implies, it is a quick cutting motion combined with very fast footwork. To perform *haya-suburi* begin in *chudan no kamae.*

A) Pushing off from the right foot, step back strongly as you raise the *shinai* overhead.

B) Push off from the left foot and step forward, cutting sharply to your own head height.

When doing *haya-suburi* quite quickly, the forward and backward steps tend to become jumps. It is important to concentrate on covering ground forward and backward rather than jumping up and down. Maintain proper footwork so that as you move backward, the left foot moves and then the right. As you move forward, the right foot moves first and then the left.

Points to observe when doing *Haya-suburi*:

- *Haya-suburi* teaches the kendoka to power the cut from the *hara* or abdomen, rather than the arms. If the arms are used, the exercise becomes extremely tiring.

  When many *haya-suburi* are done, the tendency is for the movements to become small. Concentrate on extending the arms fully at the moment of the strike.

Haya-suburi builds stamina and teaches efficiency — it is only possible to perform many repetitions if you are relaxed.

Fundamentals of partner practice

The exercises are performed with a partner, or *aite*. Some fundamentals of paired practice are:

■ *Maai* is the dynamic combination of timing and distance. It is crucial to an understanding of kendo, and is sometimes said to be the most difficult concept to master. The basic distance used in kendo is called *issoku itto no maai* which means 'one step, one cut distance'. When two kendoka are at tip-to-tip distance, either one can take one strong step forward and cut the other's head. Therefore, this position is the correct distance of engagement. If an attack is initiated from further out, it will probably miss. If an attack is made from closer in, the strike will be too deep and it will not be counted (*see also p78*).

■ *Seme* refers to forward pressure with the sword. It is one thing to be standing in front of your opponent holding a *shinai*; it is another thing entirely to be wielding your sword with the intention of striking at the first possible opening. The difference in feeling between the two translates as a difference in forward pressure. The *kensen*, or sword tip, should not waver to left or right, but maintain a constant forward threat. Think about what your sword tip is doing at all times.

■ *Zanshin* literally means 'the heart that lingers'. Following every action, you must remain aware of what has just occurred, and recognize what could happen next. *Zanshin* comes into effect following a strike. Instead of assuming that you were successful and that the fight is over, you remain aware of the entire situation and prepare to attack again, if necessary.

Kirikaeshi

Kirikaeshi, which means 'continuous cuts', is a fundamental exercise of kendo. It teaches all the basic elements of movement, striking, distance, timing, coordination and breath control, which are central to mastery of kendo. It has been said that 'all of kendo is contained in *kirikaeshi*'. After warm-ups and the *bogu* has been put on, *kirikaeshi* is generally the first exercise of every practice.

Kirikaeshi is performed with a partner, who is referred to as the *motodachi*, or receiver of the technique (*see p54*). Because this is the first part of the practice, it has a special etiquette:

1. Stand opposite your partner with your *shinai* by your left side.
2. Perform a standing bow to your partner and ask for his cooperation in training by saying 'Onegaishimasu'.
3. Bring the *shinai* up to the left hip. Place your thumb on the *tsuba*. Take three steps forward.
4. On the third step, draw the *shinai* out and mirror your partner, the tips of your *shinai* almost touching.
5. Turn your left foot inward so that your heels are almost touching. Go into a deep squat with the knees spread apart. This position is called *sonkyo*. Maintain the same straight posture with your upper body; do not lean forward. Stand up.

above *SONKYO*, FRONT AND SIDE VIEWS

You are now ready to perform *kirikaeshi*:

1. Stand up from *sonkyo*, sword tips still touching.
2. Take a deep breath, and make a strong *kiai* to gather your power.
3. Take a large step forward, and strike *shomen*, the centre of your opponent's head, with a stamping step (*fumikomu*) and a loud *kiai* of 'Men!' and immediately pull up the rear foot.
4. Continue moving forward. Bring your hands down in front of your *tanden* (lower abdomen), and strongly crash into your opponent. Your momentum will propel the opponent backward. This 'body check' is called *tai atari*; the point where you meet your opponent hand-to-hand is called *tsuba zeriai*.
5. Strike your opponent's left *men*.
6. As he steps back, immediately strike his right *men*.
   Continue striking right and left *men* alternately as he steps backward. These hits are done with a sliding step and you must *kiai* with each strike. The normal sequence is to make four hits forward, then begin striking as you move backward, hitting five times. Re-establish the correct distance, and repeat steps 1–6.
   After the second set of strikes, re-establish the correct distance and strike *men*.
7. This time, continue moving through with arms extended, beyond the opponent to a point well past his reach.
8. With *zanshin* (awareness, readiness) turn to face your opponent. Now you are the *motodachi* and will receive his techniques.

Notes
· *The white crack between kendoka on page 48 indicates that the distance between them is slightly greater than shown here.*

· *Numbers are repeated when the description under the same number refers to two moves.*

KIRIKAESHI, ALTHOUGH A FUNDAMENTAL AND APPARENTLY SIMPLE PART OF KENDO PRACTICE, INVOLVES A COMPLEX INTERPLAY BETWEEN DISTANCE, TIMING, PRESSURE, ATTACK AND DEFENCE.

Points to observe when doing *kirikaeshi:*

- The exercise can be done by striking the *men* directly, or the *motodachi* may protect his head by blocking with his *shinai*. In either case, it is essential that all strikes be directed to the correct spot — the front of the *men*, left or right of centre (*sayu men*).

- Always maintain good posture during this exercise. Do not lean forward or back.

- Maintain a steady height and do not 'gallop' as you move forward; your head should not bob up and down as you step forward. Keep the knees springy and slightly bent.

- Eventually, you should do this exercise with only two breaths and, ultimately, one breath. To do this, maintain a steady *kiai* and control your diaphragm.

Points to observe when receiving *kirikaeshi:*

- Distance is extremely important in this exercise. It is the *motodachi*'s responsibility to maintain the appropriate distance so that *shidachi* does not get too close to execute the *men* strikes with the correct arm extension. Similarly, *motodachi* must keep up with *shidachi*'s timing when moving backward.

- When blocking a strike to the head, keep your hands on your hip so that you block with the upper part of the *shinai*, which runs upward diagonally, the tip on the centreline overhead.

- When the receiver blocks a blow to the left side of the head, the *shinai* is held almost as normal in the hands, but the left hand is down by the left hip, and the right hand is near the left side (A). The *shinai* is angled so that it runs upward diagonally, with the tip on the centreline (overhead). The right hand can relax a bit.

- When blocking on the right side, the left (bottom) hand will be near the right hip (B). The *shinai* is again angled up toward the centre. If you took a double-exposure photo of the two *shinai* positions, it would look like a steeply-angled roof covering your head, with the two *shinai* tips

meeting at the peak of the roof. The point is to protect your head against cuts that are coming to the corners of your *men*.

- *Motodachi* walks backward and forward naturally, alternately crossing his feet on each step (*ayumi ashi*).

- On the final *men* cut, just after contact, the *motodachi* should step aside slightly to allow *shidachi* to move through.

WAZA TECHNIQUES

Traditionally, kendo *waza* can be divided into two general categories based on whether you initiate an attack or counter the attack. These two categories are known as *shikake-waza* and *oji-waza*. Some of the most useful techniques are described in this chapter.

When practising *waza*, one person acts as the receiver of the techniques. This person is the *motodachi*. The person who executes the *waza* is called *kakarite* or sometimes *aite*. A note about right (*migi*) and left (*hidari*): it is conventional to describe targets by referring to the opponent's anatomical right and left sides. For example, a strike to the opponent's *migi do* (right torso) is a strike that is made to the left, as seen from the attacker's perspective.

Shikake-waza

Shikake-waza (initiating a strike) are techniques used to create an opening in your opponent's *kamae*, (stance), causing his sword tip to move off the centre-line and leaving him open to an attack. When your

---

Shikake-waza (challenge techniques)

Ippon uchi no waza (basic, one-strike techniques)

Men kihon

(basic strikes to the head)

- *Shomen* — front of the head
- *Hidari men* — left of the head
- *Migi men* — right of the head

Kote kihon

(basic strikes to the wrist)

- *Migi kote* — right wrist

Do kihon

(basic strikes to the torso)

- *Migi do* — right side

Harai waza (parrying techniques)

- *Harai men* (Outside & Inside)
- *Harai kote*
- *Harai migi do*

Nidan waza (two-strike techniques)

- *Kote men*
- *Men men*
- *Kote do*
- *Men do*

Debana waza (taking advantage of the opponent's intention to attack)

- *Debana men*
- *Debana kote*

Hiki waza (stepping-back techniques)

- *Hiki men*
- *Hiki do*

opposite IN GOOD WEATHER, PRACTISING OUTDOORS CAN BE AN INTERESTING CHANGE FROM THE *DOJO*, AND GIVES THE KENDOKA A CHANCE TO TRY TERRAIN OTHER THAN HARDWOOD FLOORS.

opponent is in a strong *kamae*, you need to disrupt the *kamae* to create an opening for an attack. To exploit this opening the kendoka must move in without hesitation and strike.

Ippon uchi no waza (basic, one-strike techniques)

If your opponent offers you an opening you must exploit it. These techniques take advantage of a momentary opening, and must be done without hesitation as the opportunity to strike will not last long.

More advanced *waza* is built on these basic strikes, so it is important for beginners to master these techniques before moving on.

Men kihon (basic strikes to the head)

A. *Shomen uchi* (front of the head)

Stepping forward with your right foot you strike the centre of your opponent's *men*.

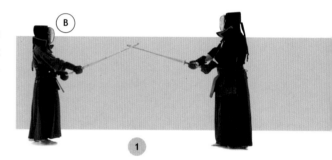

1. Both kendoka are in *chudan no kamae* (*see p40*).
2. *Motodachi* lowers the tip of the *shinai*, which creates an opening.
3. *Kakarite* swings the *shinai* overhead.
4. As *kakarite* steps out with the right foot, the strike hits the centre of *motodachi*'s *men*.
5. *Kakarite* finishes the strike and immediately brings the left foot to the right heel to re-establish correct *kamae*.
6. *Kakarite* maintains this arm position and quickly moves past *motodachi* on the right side using *okuri ashi* (*see p43*).

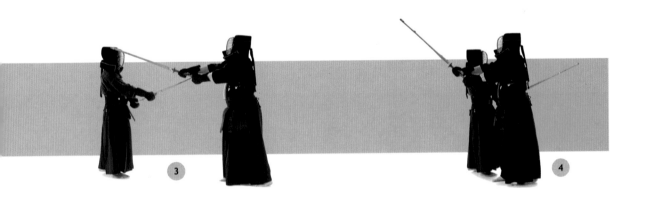

B. *Hidari men* (left of the head)

Stepping forward with your right foot, you strike the upper left corner of your opponent's *men*.

1. Both kendoka are in *chudan no kamae*. *Motodachi* lowers the tip of the *shinai (as shown in A2)*.
2. *Kakarite* swings the *shinai* up overhead.
3. As *kakarite* steps out with the right foot, the strike hits the front of *motodachi*'s *men*, left of centre.
4. *Kakarite* finishes the strike, bringing the left foot up to the right heel immediately. *Kakarite* maintains an extended arm position and moves past *motodachi* on the right, using *okuri ashi*.

C. *Migi Men* (right of the head)

Stepping forward with your right foot, strike the front of your opponent's *men*, right of centre.

1. Both kendoka are in *chudan no kamae*. *Motodachi* lowers the tip of the *shinai (as shown in A2)*.
2. *Kakarite* swings the *shinai* up overhead.
3. As *kakarite* steps out with the right foot, the strike hits the front of *motodachi*'s *men*, right of centre.
4. *Kakarite* finishes the strike, bringing the left foot up to the right immediately. *Kakarite* maintains this arm position and moves past *motodachi* on the left side, using *okuri ashi*.

Kote kihon
(basic strikes to the wrist)
A. *Migi kote* (right wrist)

Stepping forward with your right foot, you strike the right wrist of your opponent.

1. Both kendoka are in *chudan no kamae*.
2. *Motodachi* raises the tip of his *shinai* slightly, exposing his *kote* (see A2, p56). *Kakarite* swings the *shinai* overhead.
3. Stepping out with the right foot, *kakarite* simultaneously strikes *motodachi*'s right *kote*.
4. *Kakarite* immediately brings the left foot up to the right and maintains a forward arm position (*shinai* at *kote* height — that of the opponent's wrist) and moves past *motodachi* on the left side.

Although there are a few exceptions, the idea is that, after making a strike to any body part, you should maintain your *shinai* at the height of the strike. So, when you strike *men*, you hold the *shinai* at around head height; when you strike *kote*, you should hold the *shinai* at the height of the opponent's wrist. *Kote*-striking exercises are almost always going to be performed against an opponent who is in *chudan no kamae*, so this height is around waist level.

Do kihon
(basic strikes to the torso)
B. *Migi do* (right side)

Stepping forward with your right foot, you strike the right side of your opponent's *do*.

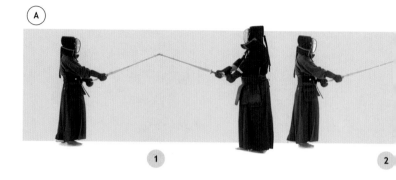

1. Both kendoka are in *chudan no kamae*.
2. *Motodachi* raises the *shinai*, exposing the *do*. *Kakarite* swings the *shinai* straight up overhead.
3. Stepping out with the right foot, *kakarite* strikes the right side of *motodachi*'s *do*.
4. *Kakarite* immediately brings the left foot up to the right heel to re-establish correct foot position, while beginning to fold the *shinai* back to the left.
5. *Kakarite* passes *motodachi* in the right side, allowing the *shinai* to fold back. Once *kakarite* moves out of range, he turns and resumes *kamae*.

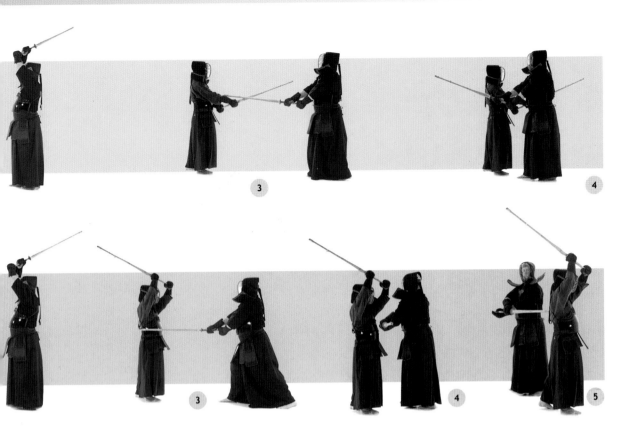

Harai waza (parrying techniques)

The term '*harai*' implies sweeping the opponent's weapon out of the way. When your opponent is in a stable and strong *kamae* and ready to counter any move you make, you may parry his *shinai* to the right or left and immediately strike the opening that this creates. You only need to move the opponent's *shinai* tip slightly off centre to create an opening. It is important to perform the parry and the subsequent attack as one continuous movement.

C. *Harai men* (outside)

Stepping forward with your right foot, you sweep the opponent's *shinai* diagonally upward to the left and strike your opponent's *men*.

1. Both kendoka are in *chudan no kamae*.
2. *Kakarite* sweeps *motodachi*'s sword up diagonallly to the left, while stepping in with the right foot. This action moves *motodachi*'s sword slightly up and off centre.
3. *Kakarite* continues this upward motion, raising the *shinai* above the head and bringing the left foot up in preparation to strike.
4. Before *motodachi* can re-establish a strong *kamae*, *kakarite* strikes the centre of *motodachi*'s *men* while stepping out with the right foot.
5. Bringing the left foot up to the right, *kakarite* then passes through on the right side.

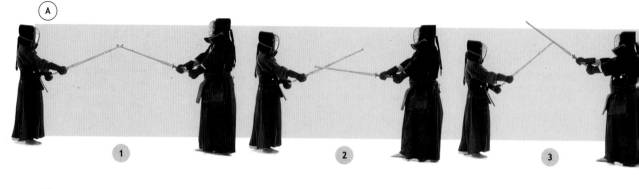

A. *Harai men* (inside)

Stepping forward with your right foot, you sweep the opponent's *shinai* diagonally upward to the right and strike your opponent's *men*.

1. Both kendoka are in *chudan no kamae*.
2. *Kakarite* takes a small step in on the right foot, moving the *shinai* under and to the left of *motodachi*'s *shinai*.
3. *Kakarite* then sweeps *motodachi*'s sword upward on a diagonal from left to right.
4. *Kakarite* continues this upward movement, raising the *shinai* overhead.
5. *Kakarite* steps forward with the right foot, while executing a *men* strike.
6. *Kakarite* continues moving past *motodachi* on the left.

B. *Harai kote*

Stepping forward with your right foot, you sweep the opponent's *shinai* diagonally to the right and strike your opponent's *kote*.

1. Both kendoka are in *chudan no kamae*.
2. *Kakarite* takes a forward step in on the right foot and lowers the *shinai* slightly.

3. *Kakarite* then sweeps *motodachi*'s sword diagonally up and to the right, using a small semicircular motion.
4. From this raised *shinai* position, *kakarite* immediately strikes down onto *motodachi*'s *kote*.
5. Bringing the left foot up to the right, *kakarite* then passes *motodachi* on the left.

C. *Harai migi do*

Stepping forward with your right foot, you sweep the opponent's *shinai* in a circular motion diagonally upward to the right and strike the opponent's right *do*.

1. Both kendoka are in *chudan no kamae*.
2. *Kakarite* takes a small step in on the right foot, at the same moment dropping the *shinai* under that of *motodachi*, so that it is positioned along the left side of the opponent's sword.
3. *Kakarite* slides the *shinai* against that of *motodachi* in a strong circular motion, parrying *motodachi*'s *shinai* diagonally upward and to the right. *Motodachi* may attempt to recover and prepare to counterattack.
4. Before *motodachi* can move, *kakarite* continues the motion of the *shinai*, striking *motodachi*'s right *do*.
5. *Kakarite* moves past *motodachi* on the left.

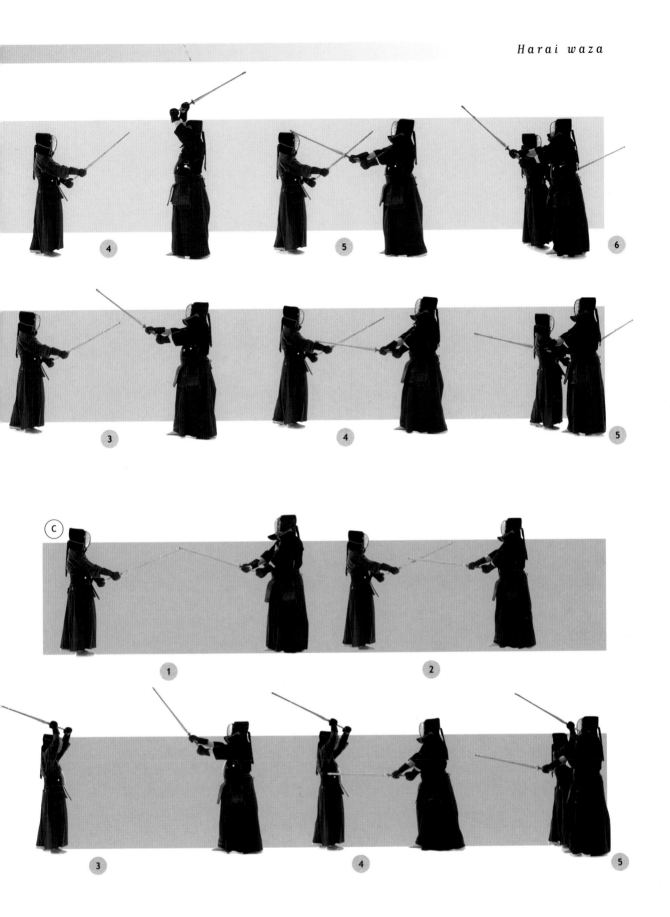

Nidan waza (two-strike techniques)

Nidan waza is a technique of delivering two strikes consecutively. The first strike often serves to disrupt the opponent's stance, eliciting a reaction and creating an opening for the second strike to score a successful hit. Another situation arises when both kendoka strike simultaneously (*ai-uchi*, where the two strikes cancel each other), but one player continues immediately with a second strike. It is important that these two strikes are performed continuously, with no pause between them.

A. *Kote men*

Stepping forward, you strike the opponent's right wrist, then as the opponent steps back, you follow immediately with a strike to the head. Maintain the correct striking distance by taking small steps — do not allow yourself to move in too deeply.

1. Both kendoka are in *chudan no kamae*.
2. The attacker sees an opening in the opponent's *kote*, and strikes the right wrist.
3. The opponent reacts by stepping back slightly, exposing the head.
4. Maintaining forward pressure, the attacker immediately strikes *men* and then follows through on the left side.

B. *Men men*

Stepping forward, you strike the centre of the opponent's head. The opponent reacts by moving backward; you immediately strike the head again.

1. Both kendoka are in *chudan no kamae*.
2. The attacker sees an opening and strikes the centre of the opponent's *men*.
3. The opponent moves back, trying to avoid the strike. The opponent's *kamae* is disrupted, further opening the head.
4. Maintaining forward pressure, the attacker immediately strikes *men* a second time and follows through on the right.

C. *Kote do*

Stepping forward, you strike at the wrist of your opponent, who moves back, while preparing to strike back by lifting the *shinai*. This opens the opponent's *do*, which you strike immediately.

1. Both kendoka are in *chudan no kamae*.
2. The attacker sees an opening and strikes for the opponent's wrist. The attacker maintains a strong pressure forward, forcing the opponent up and back.
3. The opponent raises the *shinai*, either to block the next attack, or to counterattack. The opponent's *do* becomes exposed.
4. At this precise moment, the attacker takes the opponent's left *do*.
5. The attacker passes through on the right side.

A. *Men do*

Stepping forward, you strike at your opponent's head. The opponent reacts by raising the *shinai*, thus exposing the *do*; you strike at your opponent's *do* immediately.

1. Both kendoka are in *chudan no kamae*.
2. You see an opening and strike at your opponent's head. Maintaining a strong pressure forward, you threaten with a second strike to the *men*.
3. Your opponent lifts the *shinai* in an attempt to block or counterattack.
4. At this point, you strike the exposed *do*. (This can be executed on the left or right side.)
5. You pass through on the right side.

Debana waza (taking advantage of the opponent's intention to attack)

Debana waza techniques are used to strike your opponent at the moment you realize that the attacker is about to strike. Observing the shift in posture, and anticipating the attack to come, you move in and strike, taking advantage of your opponent's momentary inability to respond. These *waza* require a great deal of practice to execute correctly because you must be able to read your opponent's intentions and catch the subtle movement before the attack.

B. *Debana men*

At the moment your opponent attempts to strike, you catch the movement and launch forward to strike the opponent's *men*.

1. Both kendoka are in *chudan no kamae*.
2. Your attacker begins the attempted strike, but you see the movement and immediately raise your *shinai*, pushing it forward toward the centre of your attacker's *men*.
3. Before your attacker can strike, you quickly strike the centre of your *opponent*'s *men*.
4. You pass through on the left.

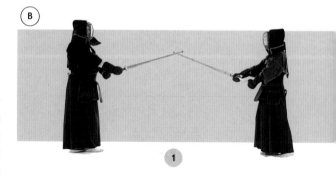

There must be no hesitation; the moment you see your attacker move, you must strike the *men* and defeat your opponent's timing.

C. Debana kote

At the moment your opponent attempts to move forward and strike, you catch the movement and launch forward, striking the exposed *kote*.

1. Both kendoka are in *chudan no kamae*.
2. Your attacker begins a movement forward to strike your *men*, but as soon as you see this movement you

immediately lift your *shinai* slightly, extending it toward your attacker's *kote*.

3. At the moment the *kote* becomes exposed, you strike it before your opponent has a chance to strike your *men*. Note that *kote* is closer than *men*. This gives you the advantage of distance over your opponent.

4. Continue moving through on the left side using proper *suri ashi* (see p43).

Again there must be no hesitation. Raising the *shinai* to strike will inevitably expose your opponent's *kote*. At this moment you must strike.

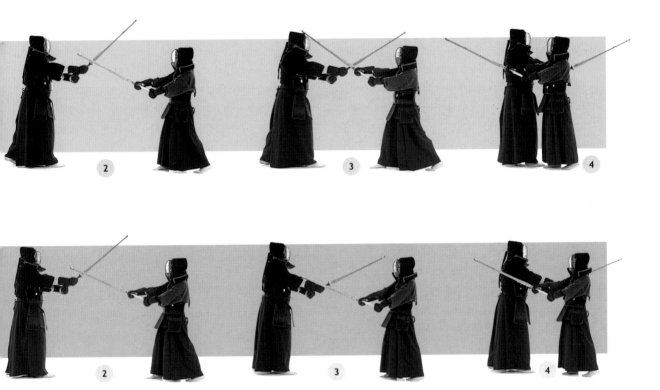

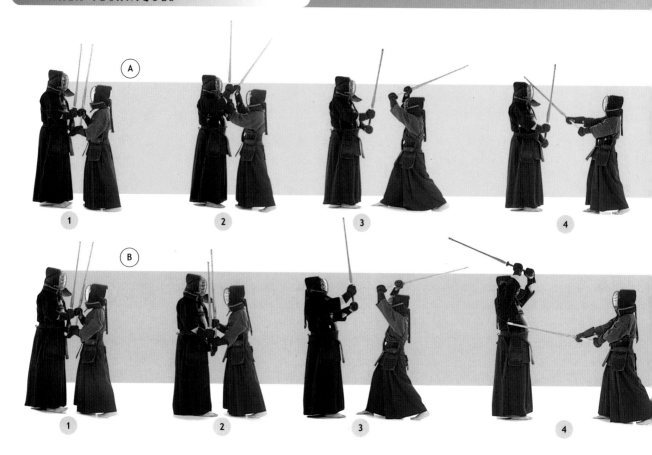

Hiki waza
(stepping-back techniques)

Hiki waza are techniques for hitting when you are very close to your opponent. These techniques can be performed in various ways, but in this section they will be described from the *tsuba zeriai* position (*see p50*). These techniques work by upsetting your opponent's balance through the use of *tai atari* (body checking *see p50*), to create the space and an opening to strike. Start these techniques from a *tsuba zeriai* position by standing close to your opponent, hands held low in front of your hips and your *shinai* almost vertical, protecting your own head.

A. *Hiki men*

From *tsuba zeriai* you push off your opponent, at the same time moving back, creating enough distance to strike. Your opponent's *shinai* may drop while moving back, exposing the head. At this moment you strike the opponent's *men*.

1. Both kendoka are in *tsuba zeriai*.

2. Push off your opponent's *tsuka*.

3. Quickly step back with the left foot and create enough space to strike your opponent, while raising your *shinai*.

4. Your opponent may step forward or allow the *shinai* to waver, exposing the *men*. At this moment strike *men* with a stamp of the right foot.

5. With your *shinai* raised high overhead, continue moving back in a straight line using proper *suri ashi*.

6. When you are out of *motodachi*'s range, return to *chudan no kamae*.

You may coerce your opponent into exposing *men* by pushing up on your opponent's *shinai* as you push off and move back. *Motodachi* may overcompensate by lowering the hands, and thereby exposing the *men*.

B. *Hiki do*

From *tsuba zeriai* you push off your opponent, at the same time moving back, creating enough distance to strike. At this point your opponent's *shinai* may rise, opening the *do*. Strike *motodachi*'s *do*.

1. Both kendoka are in *tsuba zeriai*.
2. Push off your opponent's *tsuka*.
3. Quickly step back with the left foot and create enough space to strike your opponent, while raising your *shinai*.
4. Your opponent may raise the *shinai* to block or strike *men*; at this moment strike the exposed right *do* as you stamp with the right foot.
5. Continue moving back in a straight line using proper *suri ashi*, holding the *shinai* high above your head.
6. When out of range, return to *chudan no kamae*.

You may coerce your opponent into exposing the *do* by pushing down on your opponent's *shinai* as you push off and move back. *Motodachi* may overcompensate by raising the hands, thereby exposing *do*.

Oji waza

Responding techniques (*oji waza*) allow kendoka to parry and counterattack simultaneously. It is important that the counterattacks be made quickly without pausing in order to be successful.

Oji waza (responding techniques)

Nuki waza (avoiding strike by moving the target)	Kaeshi waza (parrying block and counterattack)
■ Kote nuki men	■ Men kaeshi men
■ Kote nuki kote	■ Men kaeshi do

1   2

Nuki waza

Nuki waza are techniques that allow you to avoid your opponent's strike by moving the intended target out of the line of strike at the moment that the *kakarite* commits to hitting. Simultaneously you strike before *kakarite* can recover from the failed attack.

A. *Kote nuki men*

The opponent attempts to strike your *kote*. You respond by removing your *kote* from the striking line and hit your opponent's *men*.

1. Both kendoka start in *chudan no kamae*.

2. The attacker starts to move in and tries to attack your *kote*.

1   2

B. *Kote nuki kote*

The opponent attempts to strike your *kote*. You remove your *kote* from the striking line and then strike *kakarite*'s *kote*.

1. Both kendoka are in *chudan no kamae*.

2. The attacker starts to move in and tries to strike at your *kote*.

3. Seeing this attack coming, you shift slightly to the left while moving your *shinai* in a downward semicircle.

4. You avoid the strike and come up on the left side of the opponent's *shinai*.

5. Continue this movement and strike *kakarite*'s *kote*.

6. Follow through on a straight line moving with proper *suri ashi*.

3   4   5

3. You see this attack and quickly raise your *shinai*, avoiding *kakarite*'s *kote* strike.
4. Step forward and hit your opponent's exposed *men*.
5. Continue moving through on a straight line using proper *suri ashi*.

If the attacker moves in deeply to strike, then you will need to take a step back as you raise your *shinai* in order to fully avoid *kakarite*'s strike.

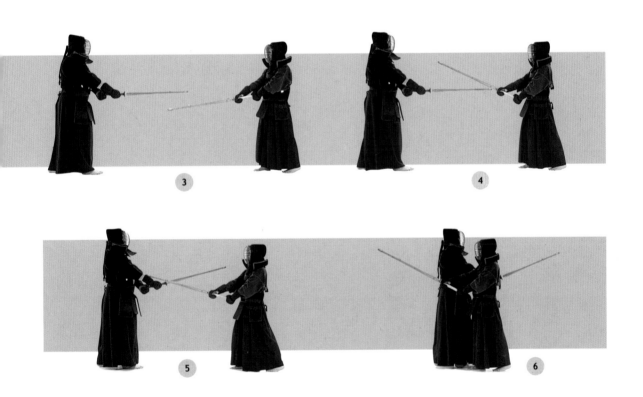

3   4

5   6

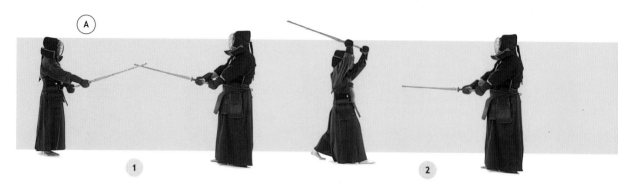

Kaeshi waza

Kaeshi waza are techniques that involve a large parrying block and counterattack that uses some of the momentum of the deflection of the attacker's strike to aid in your return strike. A characteristic of *kaeshi waza* is the way the *shinai* flips sides as it deflects and then strikes. For example, if you block your opponent's attack on the right, swing the *shinai* around and forward and attack to the left. These techniques are used when you are late in spotting your opponent's intentions.

A. *Men kaeshi men*

The opponent strikes at your *men*. You parry this attack and counter to *kakarite*'s left or right *men*. It can be done on either side, but this example describes it done on the right, from *kakarite*'s perspective.

1. Both kendoka are in *chudan no kamae*.
2. The attacker prepares to move in and strike *men*.
3. Seeing this attack, you begin to raise your *shinai*, at the same time pushing the left hand out to the right side. Use this slanted *shinai* to block your own head as you continue to lift your hands, making contact with *motodachi*'s *shinai*.
4. *Motodachi*'s *shinai* is deflected slightly off line, while you continue the sword motion upward.
5. In one continuous motion redirect the momentum of your *shinai*, bringing the tip back and to the right.
6. Smoothly continue this motion of the *shinai* as you strike forward to *motodachi*'s left *men*.
7. Move past your opponent on the right side.

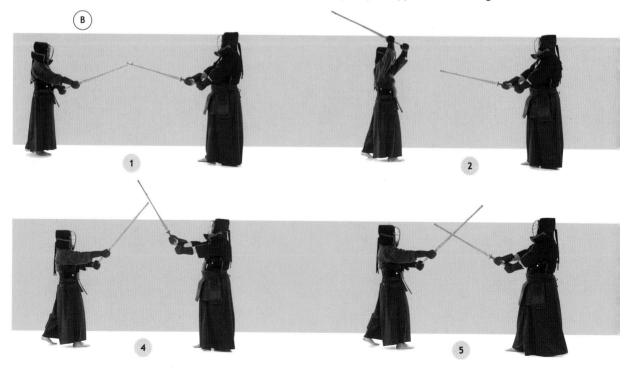

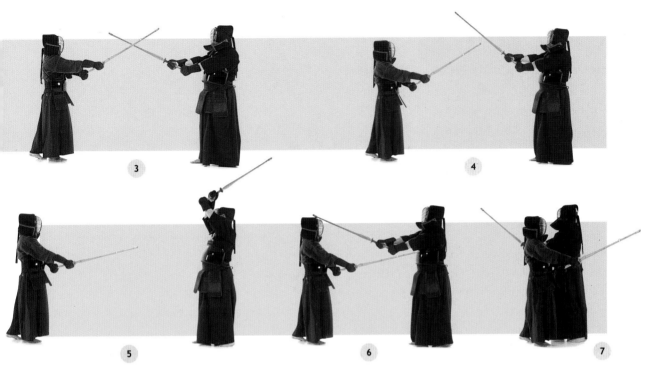

3   4

5   6   7

B. *Men kaeshi do*

The opponent strikes at your *men*, you parry this attack, and strike the left or right *do*. This technique can also be performed on either side; here, it is described done to the left, from *kakarite*'s perspective.

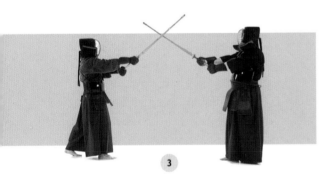

3

1. Both kendoka are in *chudan no kamae*.
2. The attacker prepares to move in and strike *men*.
3. Seeing the attack you begin to raise your *shinai*, at the same time bringing your left hand out to the left side. Use this slanted *shinai* to block your own head as you continue to lift your hands, making contact with *motodachi*'s *shinai*.
4. *Motodachi*'s *shinai* is deflected slightly off line, while you continue the sword motion upward.
5. In one continuous motion redirect the momentum of your *shinai* bringing the tip around and to the left.
6. Smoothly continue this *shinai* motion as you strike forward to *Motodachi*'s right *do*. Step forward if necessary to establish the correct distance.
7. Move past your opponent on the right side.

6   7

KEIKO

The word *keiko* means 'practice' in general terms, but in the context of kendo, it has the additional connotation of a sparring match. Keiko is your opportunity to put into practice all the principles and techniques you have learned.

Kakari geiko

Kakari geiko is the practice of all-out attacking. The kendoka doing *kakari geiko* give no thought to their defence but pour all their energy into repeatedly attacking any available open targets on the opponent. Regardless of the success or failure of each technique, they concentrate entirely on the next attack, executing all strikes vigorously and with a loud *kiai*. The kendoka continue until they are completely exhausted.

Kakari geiko can be done with two practitioners of roughly equal level, in which case they attack each other with equal aggression. It can also be done with students of unequal levels of skill. In this case, the upper-level student acts as *motodachi*, and receives the attacks of the other. The *motodachi* must reveal openings by exposing, for example, his *kote*; the partner must be able to spot the opening and attack immediately.

Kakari geiko serves two main purposes. Firstly, it teaches the kendoka not to hold back, but to seize and exploit opportunities immediately, without having to think about it or assess the situation first. Kendoka who lack this ability and fight too conservatively will not be able to exploit openings in a match.

Secondly, *kakari geiko* is gruelling. Kendoka push themselves to the limit of endurance, and beyond. The player must concentrate on keeping correct form and not allowing his technique to fall apart due to exhaustion. This not only builds physical stamina, but teaches the player to break through his self-imposed mental barriers.

Gokaku geiko

Gokaku geiko is practice between two players with roughly equal levels of skill. It is more conservative than *kakari geiko*. Players should attempt techniques about which they feel most confident, trying to score hits without giving up points. It is also an opportunity to experiment with new techniques.

Shobu geiko

Shobu geiko is an informal bout. There is no judge, so the players must be sportsmanlike and mutually agree when an attack is effective. The duration of the session can be agreed to by the players. For example, a bout may be set for two points, or five minutes, whichever comes first. Although it is informal, *shobu geiko* is a chance to practise in a competitive environment where you must call upon your skills of attack and defence.

Kendo tai kai (tournament)

The goal of kendo, in one sense, is to test your skill against that of your opponent. Tournaments are the proving ground of your abilities — a chance to see whether you can best your opponent in a high-pressure situation. Despite the increased pressure and higher stakes, however, you will do your best if you approach every match with the same attitude as a regular practice. The other side of the coin is equally important: you should approach all your practices as if they were important matches! When the time comes to participate in a tournament, you should be familiar with the rules of the event.

opposite KEIKO IS AN OPPORTUNITY TO TEST YOUR SKILLS AGAINST THOSE OF AN OPPONENT AND DISCOVER YOUR OWN STRENGTHS AND WEAKNESSES.

SHINAI BLUR AS TWO KENDOKA MOVE IN FOR AN ATTACK. REFEREES NEED TO BE VERY SKILLED TO CALL MATCH POINTS ACCURATELY.

Structure

Matches are conducted in a square or rectangular court, each side measuring between 9m (30ft) and 11m (36ft). Three referees (*shinpan*) preside over a match: one chief referee and two sub-referees. Each player is assigned a marker, either red or white, which is tied to the cords of the *men*. Each referee has a red and a white flag. When a referee observes a strike that satisfies the requirements for a point, that referee raises the flag of the corresponding colour. For a point to be scored, at least two of the three referees must agree that a strike was effective.

The match

Competitors begin a match standing outside the court with their *shinai* held in their left hand, hanging by their side. At the signal from the chief referee, each competitor makes a small bow and enters the court, raising the *shinai* to the left hip. They take three steps up to a line marked on the floor. On the third step, the players draw out their *shinai* and match blades as they drop into *sonkyo* (*see p49 and glossary*).

The centre of the court is marked with an X on the floor; the tips of the competitors' *shinai* will meet over this X. At the moment that both competitors stand, the chief referee calls *'Hajime!'* (start) and the match begins.

Matches are typically scheduled for two points or five minutes. Whoever achieves two points first, or whoever is ahead at the end of five minutes, is the winner.

After one point has been scored, the referees will order the players to stop, and they will return to their original positions. The match will then continue until another point is scored, or time runs out. Once the match is over and the players have returned to their original positions, they match blades, assume *sonkyo*, and return their sword to the left hip. Standing up, they take three steps back, and step out of the court, making a small bow.

If the match is tied at the end of five minutes, the match may be declared a draw, or an overtime period may be stipulated. The first person to score in overtime wins the match.

Referees' rules and calls

A referee's most important job is to determine whether an individual strike should be counted for a point, or not. Referees are experienced kendoka with significant knowledge of the sport and, therefore, what constitutes a valid strike. In general, for a strike to be considered valid and be counted for a point, it must satisfy the following conditions:

■ It must be executed with the correct posture and expression of *ki-ken-tai-ichi* (*see p47*). In other words, the strike, a correct foot stamp, and a powerful *kiai* must all happen at the same instant.

DODGING OUT OF THE WAY OF A STRIKE INTENDED FOR HIS *MEN*, THE PLAYER ON THE RIGHT NARROWLY MISSES SCORING A POINT ON HIS OPPONENT'S *DO*.

- Strikes which are made simultaneously, by both attacker and defender, cancel each other out and do not count.
- The strike must be made with the correct part of the *shinai*: the section from the *nakayui* forward, called the *datotsu-bu* (*see p16*).
- The strike must be made with the cutting edge of the *shinai* (opposite the *tsuru* string).
- The strike must be made accurately to the correct target. All the targets discussed so far (*men, do, kote,* and *tsuki, see p48*) count as targets with the following exceptions:
    - Only the top centre, and upper corners of the *men* count, not the sides of the head (cutting close to the ears is dangerous).
    - Striking the metal grille does not count.
    - Only the wrist counts; striking the hand does not count, nor strikes that touch the *tsuba* (*see p16*).
    - The opponent's left wrist is an acceptable target only when they are in *jodan no kamae* (*see p41*).
    - A *tsuki* (*see p45*) is only acceptable to the small pad on the opponents's *men* that covers the throat.
- Strikes must be made with a follow-through motion forward, or backward if performed from *tsuba zeriai* (*see p50*); following the strike, the kendoka must exhibit correct *zanshin* (*see p49*) and readiness.

Fouls

Referees also rule on fouls. Examples of fouls would be stepping out of bounds, pushing an opponent excessively, grabbing an opponent's *shinai*, tripping the opponent, and other behaviour which is considered unsportsmanlike or against the rules. You must obey the referee's decisions at all times. Commission of a foul results in the opponent receiving a half-point; two such fouls give the opponent a full point and could result in the match being called.

Common commands and calls

Referees' calls are made in Japanese, reflecting the origins of the art.

Call	Meaning
Hajime	Begin
Yame	Stop
Wakare	The players must separate and reset at tip-to-tip distance
Torikeshi	A previously called point is cancelled
Encho	Time extension
Shobu ari	The match has been decided; one side has won
Hikiwake	The match is a draw
Gogi	The referees call a conference
Hansoku	A half-point penalty is applied

KENDO NO KATA

An introduction

The *Kendo no Kata* (set forms of kendo) were established in 1912 by a committee of expert swordsmen from a number of different schools of swordsmanship. Their goal was to create a standardized set of techniques that could be studied by all kendoka, regardless of where they were or their affiliation.

In this section, we will present the first three *kata* of the 10 ZNKR Kendo Kata. They are quite detailed, so a full description of all 10 would be beyond the scope of this book. Mastery of the first three, however, will enable beginning kendoka to challenge their first grading.

Uchidachi and shidachi

In *kata* practice, there are two roles. The first is that of *uchidachi*, who initiates the movements in the *kata* and controls the combative distance by choosing when to attack. The *shidachi* responds to *uchidachi*'s movements with counterattacks.

In *kata*, *shidachi* always 'wins' in the sense that *shidachi*'s techniques are successful. *Kata*, however, are not competitive. This is a cooperative training method that is infused with fighting spirit. Although the moves are choreographed, both *shidachi* and *uchidachi* should approach every *kata* with the attitude that, should the situation change suddenly, each would be ready to respond appropriately. Without this spirit, *kata* practice is merely a waltz where each person moves without reference to the partner.

Etiquette

Before beginning the forms hold the *bokuto* (*see p16*) with the edge up, in your right hand (A). Turn to face your partner at a distance of about nine paces. Partners bow to each other to a depth of no more than 30 degrees from vertical (B).

Straighten up and, holding the *bokuto* in front of your body, pass it to your left hand (C), and place it on the left hip (D). The thumb comes up to the *tsuba*. With a real *katana* this controls the sword in the scabbard.

Both partners take three steps in toward the centre. Drawing the sword out (E) and up (F), they come to *issoku itto no maai*, or one-step cutting distance. The tips of the swords move down and match so that they are just crossing. Lower yourself into *sonkyo*, a deep squat with the knees spread (G). Do not move your upper body. Stand up (H).

Both partners lower their swords to the position of no advantage, called *kamae o toku,* which means the release of the stance (*see p41*). It is similar to *gedan* except that the sword is rolled slightly outward, signifying a subtle lowering of aggression (I). Take five small steps backward, returning to your original starting position. Raise your swords to *chudan no kamae* (J).

Note on walking

There are two basic methods of moving: *okuri ashi* (a slide step where the feet do not cross), and *ayumi ashi* (a natural walking step where the feet cross with each step) *see p47*. These terms will be used extensively in the descriptions to follow.

Distances

Maai is a Japanese term that refers to the distance between opponents. In the context of Kendo there are three types of *maai*: *toi maai* (furthest away from each other), *issoku itto no maai* (at which most action takes place), and *chikai maai* (the closest).

Ippon-me: Kata number one

This *kata* is a formal version of *nuki men* (*see p80*).

Uchidachi attempts to strike *shidachi*'s *men*. *Shidachi* evades the cut, and counters with a *men* cut of his own.

Shidachi

1. From *chudan* (A) respond immediately to *uchidachi*'s stance by raising your sword into right *jodan* stance (B).
2. Starting with the right foot, walk forward three steps, finishing with your right foot forward (C).
3. At the instant the opponent begins to attack, sharply step back with the left foot (*okuri ashi*), avoiding the attack and allowing the sword to pass in front of you (D). Step forward with the right foot and cut to *uchidachi*'s *shomen* with the *kiai* 'Toh!' (E).
4. Lower the tip of your sword from your opponent's head to the eyes (F). Take a cautious half-slide step back (*okuri ashi*) and straighten your posture.
5. With a feeling of strong *seme* (see p49), step forward with the left foot, raising the sword up to left *jodan* (G).
6. With a strong feeling of *zanshin* (see p49), step back with the left foot as you lower the sword to *chudan* (H). Your right foot is now forward.

Uchidachi

1. From *chudan* (A), step forward with the left foot and take left *jodan* stance*[1] (B).
2. Starting with the left foot*[2], walk forward three steps to finish with your left foot forward (C).
3. Pause, looking for an opportunity to attack. Sensing an opening, step forward with the right foot and strike with the intention of cutting through the opponent's hands, head, and body. Make a strong *kiai* of 'Yah!' (D). Finish with the sword tip down, leaning slightly forward from the momentum of your failed attack.
4. Take a cautious small slide step back with the left foot (*okuri ashi*) and straighten your posture (F).
5. Take another small slide step back (*okuri ashi*) (G).
6. Cautiously raise your sword from *gedan* level to *chudan* (H).

Both lower their swords to knee level (I), rolling the hands slightly so that the edge points to the left (*kamae o toku*). They take five small steps back (J) and raise the swords to *chudan no kamae* in preparation for the next *kata*.

Footnotes to the first *kata*

*[1]Right and left *jodan*

There are two different jodan stances: right and left. In competitive or regular play (that is, everything that's not kata), left jodan is usually adopted. But in the kata, uchidachi and shidachi take opposite jodan stances. So it's important to distinguish between them.

Essentially, the difference is in which foot is forward, but there are some subtle differences regarding sword angle, too. In left jodan, the sword is angled slightly. The left hand should be directly in line with the left foot. *This creates an angle in the sword as seen from the front. In right jodan, the hands are centred and the sword is straight up and down, as seen from the front.*

*[2] Footwork

Starting right foot forward, you take a step onto your left foot as you raise the sword to jodan. Then you step forward again with the left. The feet in jodan aren't that far apart, so it's not too difficult to step forward with the left, although it might seem unnatural to a beginner.

Nihon-me: Kata number two

This *kata* is a formal version of *nuki kote* (*see p82*). *Uchidachi* attempts to strike *shidachi*'s *kote*, but *shidachi* evades with a diagonal motion and cuts *uchidachi*'s *kote*.

Shidachi

1. Remaining in *chudan* (A), take three steps to the centre, finishing with your right foot forward. Match blades with *uchidachi* (B).

2. At the instant that *uchidachi* begins the attack (C), step diagonally back and to the left with the left foot to avoid the strike. At the same time, drop your own blade to *gedan*-like position as you step out of the way (D).

3. Raise the sword in a large motion (E). Step back in with the right foot as you strike *uchidachi*'s right *kote*, shouting 'Toh!' (F).

4. Maintaining forward pressure and *zanshin*, step cautiously back onto the centre line (G). As *uchidachi* steps back, match blades (H).

Uchidachi

1. Beginning in *chudan* (A), take three steps to the centre, finishing with your right foot forward. Match blades with *shidachi*, tips of the swords just crossing (B).

2. Pause and, sensing an opportunity to attack, raise the sword overhead, step forward with the right foot and cut (C) for *shidachi*'s right wrist (D), shouting 'Yah!' Finish the cut at *shidachi*'s wrist level (the level of shidachi's waist), bokuto parallel to the floor.

3. *Shidachi* evades your cut (E) and returns with a *kote* cut (F).

4. Realizing that you are defeated, step back with the left foot (*okuri ashi*) (G). Raise your sword to *chudan*, matching blades with *shidachi* (H).

The opponents are now in the centre, blades matched in *chudan no kamae*. From *chudan*, both *uchidachi* and *shidachi* lower their swords to *kamae o toku* (I). Both take five small steps back (J) to the starting position and raise their swords to *chudan no kamae* (K) in preparation for the next *kata*.

Shidachi   Uchidachi

A

B

C

D

E

F

G

H

I

J

K

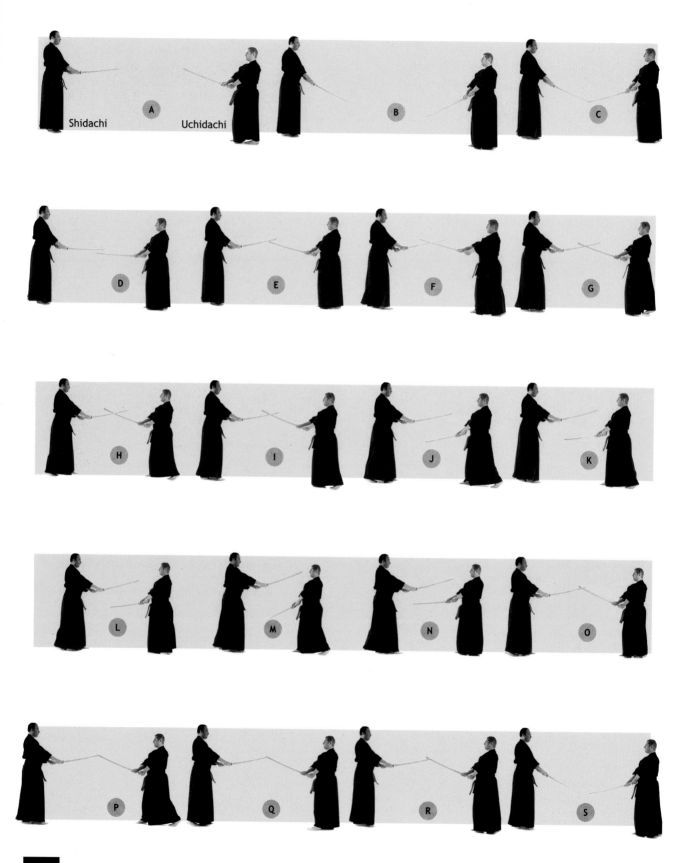

Shidachi   Uchidachi

A

B

C

D

E

F

G

H

I

J

K

L

M

N

O

P

Q

R

S

Sanbon-me: Kata number three

This *kata* is a struggle for control of the centre line, and shows the importance of *seme* and control of your opponent's sword.

Shidachi

1. Beginning in *chudan no kamae* (A), lower your *bokuto* to *gedan no kamae* (B) in response to *uchidachi*'s movement. Take three steps to the centre, right foot forward, and match blades, tips just crossing (C).

2. As *uchidachi* slowly raises his sword (D), match his movements until you both reach *chudan no kamae*. At the instant that *uchidachi* attacks, step back with the left foot (*okuri ashi*) (F) and negate the thrust by turning your *bokuto*'s edge to the right, keeping its tip on the centre line. This action absorbs the energy of *uchidachi*'s thrust while maintaining your control of the centre line.

3. Seize the initiative and thrust straight into *uchidachi*'s *suigetsu* (solar plexus) with the *kiai* '*Toh!*' as you slide forward with the right foot (G).

4. Maintain your control of the centre as you walk forward onto the left foot (*ayumi ashi*) (H). The sword tip is at the level of *uchidachi*'s chest, threatening the throat.

5. Take three steps forward (*ayumi ashi*), starting with the right foot (I, L, M). Move in on *uchidachi*, raising the sword to threaten the eyes. Do this with a strong sense of *zanshin*.

6. Pause, then take two steps back, starting with the left foot (N), and cautiously lower the tip from the opponent's face to *chudan no kamae* (O).

7. Match blades with *uchidachi* and smoothly take three steps back to the centre position (P, Q, R).

Uchidachi

1. Beginning in *chudan no kamae* (A), lower your *bokuto* to *gedan no kamae* (B). Take three steps in to the centre, finishing with your right foot forward, and matching blades with your opponent so that the tips just cross (still in *gedan no kamae*) (C).

2. With a feeling of *seme*, slowly raise the *bokuto* (D) until you reach *chudan no kamae* (E). Sensing an opening, step in with the right foot (*okuri ashi*) and thrust forward (F) by rolling your hands so that the edge of your *bokuto* faces to your right, and its curve carries it around *shidachi*'s *bokuto*. Shout '*Yah!*'

3. Respond to *shidachi*'s counterattack by stepping back with the right foot (*ayumi ashi*) (G) and attempting to retake centre. Make a small clockwise circle with the tip, bringing your sword to the left of *shidachi*'s blade. Your body is turned slightly to the right.

4. Your attempt to take centre proving unsuccessful, cross-step again with the left foot and try to take centre again (H), this time with a small counterclockwise circle that brings your sword to the right of *shidachi*'s blade. Your body is turned slightly to the left.

5. Overcome by the pressure exerted by *shidachi*, gradually lower your blade to *gedan*, as you take three steps back, left(I)-right(L)-left(M) (*ayumi ashi*).

6. Wait for *shidachi* to move back (N). As he does, cautiously raise the sword to *chudan no kamae* and match blades with *shidachi* (O).

7. Move smoothly with *shidachi*, taking three steps back to the centre (P, Q, R).

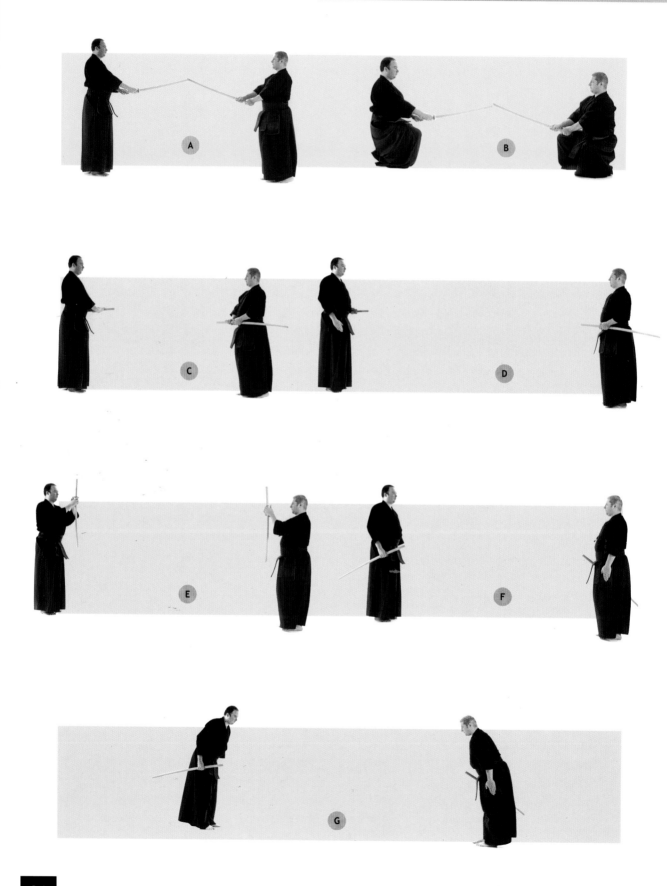

Finishing a Kata

If you are going to continue with more *kata*, drop your sword into *kamae o toku* and return to your starting position.

If the *kata* are finished, do the etiquette ritual in reverse order. Match blades (A), assume *sonkyo* (B).

Return the sword to the left hip and stand up (C). Take five steps back to the original position (D). Pass the sword in front of your body (E) to your right hand. Allow the sword to hang down by your right side (F) and bow to your partner (G).

KENDO *KATA* ARE OFTEN PERFORMED FOR DEMONSTRATIONS, AND ALSO MAKE AN INTEGRAL PART OF KENDO GRADINGS. IN THE CASE OF A DEMONSTRATION, THE FIRST AND LAST BOWS WOULD BE MADE TO THE AUDIENCE; IN A GRADING, BEGIN AND END BY BOWING TO THE JUDGES. HOLDING THE *BOKUTO* IN YOUR RIGHT HAND, PERFORM A BOW OF BETWEEN 20 AND 30 DEGREES, KEEPING THE BACK STRAIGHT AND BENDING FROM THE WAIST.

GRADING — SHINSA

Grading in kendo is voluntary and there are people who have no desire to achieve a rank. Others look forward with great enthusiasm to each opportunity to prove themselves. Grading is also a chance to measure your progress against a standard. Most tournaments have divisions based on the players' ranks, so grading will ensure that you face people with a similar level of skill and experience.

When you are ready in terms of the required age, the length of time you have been practising, and your ability as judged by your *sensei*, you may apply to your national federation for permission to take the examination for the next grade. You will have to pay a fee, which goes toward supporting the activities of your organization.

The test will follow a basic format, although it may vary slightly from place to place. The first part of the examination is *keiko*. You will be paired with an opponent who is also challenging for a higher rank. A panel of judges will examine both at the same time, assessing form and mastery of the basic techniques. Usually, keiko will be in 'ladder' format: those challenging grade are lined up, often from youngest to oldest. Player one fights player two, then player two fights player three, and so on. The last player then fights player one again. In this manner, the judges can observe everyone for two matches.

During these matches, you need to show your best kendo: vigorous attacks, well-executed strikes, proper posture, knowledge of distance and timing, control of your opponent, and mastery of *waza*. Gradings are not quite like tournament-style matches. The aim is not to win at any cost, but to display your best form.

The second component of grading is the demonstration of *Kendo no Kata*. The number of required techniques for each grade depends on the level and varies from country to country. In a grading situation, you will be grouped by rank and lined up in two rows. One row will be designated *uchidachi* (the attacker) and the other row will be *shidachi* (the defender). Everyone will do the required techniques together. Depending on the grade, the roles may be reversed so that the judges can observe everyone executing both roles.

Techniques required per grade

The number of Kendo no Kata techniques required for each grade depends on the level and varies from country to country. This table can serve as a rough guide.

Rank applied for	Required Techniques
Ikkyu (1st kyu)	Tachi (long sword) numbers 1—3
Shodan (1st dan)	Tachi numbers 1—5
Nidan (2nd dan)	Tachi numbers 1—7
Sandan (3rd dan) and up	Tachi 1—7 and Kodachi (short sword) 1—3

NATIONAL AND INTERNATIONAL FEDERATIONS

INTERNATIONAL KENDO
FEDERATION (IKF)
2nd fl., Yasukuni Kudan Minami Bldg.
2-3-14, Kudan Minami, Chiyoda-ku,
Tokyo, Japan 102-0074
Tel: 81-3-3234-6271
Fax: 81-3-3234-6007

AFRICA
SOUTH AFRICA
South African Kendo Federation
38 Knox St., Waverley,
Johannesburg 2090, South Africa
Buster Sefor (President)
sefor@icon.co.za
www.kendo.org.za

ASIA
HONG KONG
Hong Kong Kendo Association Limited
Room 1029, Sports House,
No. 1 Stadium Path, So Kon Po,
Causeway Bay, Hong Kong
hkka@hksdb.org.hk (HKKA),
www.hongkongkendo.com
Po Kit Wong (President),
JAPAN
All Japan Kendo Federation
2nd fl., Yasukuni Kudan Minami Bldg.,
2-3-14, Kudan Minami, Chiyoda-ku,
Tokyo, Japan 102-0074
jimukyoku@kendo.or.jp
www.kendo.or.jp
Yoshimitsu Takeyasu (President)
KOREA
Korea Kumdo Association
Room 505, 88 Olympic Center,
Oryun-Dong, Songpa-Gu,

Seoul, Korea 138-749
kumdo@sports.or.kr
www.kumdo.org
Jae-Wook Lee (President)
MACAO
Associacao de Kendo de Macau
Address: Caixa Postal 1784, Macau
admin@macaukendo.org
http://macaukendo.org
Mak Keng Cham (President)
MALAYSIA
Malaysia Kendo Association
22, Jalan Setiajaya,
Damansara Heights, 50490,
Kuala Lumpur, Malaysia
Abdullah M Baginda (President)
baginda@pop.jaring.my
ROC (TAIWAN)
Republic of China Kendo Association
No. 15, Chu Lun Street, Taipei
Taiwan R.O.C.
Hsiang-Lo Wu (President)
wchiaoyh@ms33.hinet.net
SINGAPORE
Singapore Kendo Club
163-D Upper East Coast Road,
Singapore 455264
chinong@singnet.com.sg
www.singaporekendo.org.sg
Chan Cheow Lin (President)
THAILAND
Thailand Kendo Club
84/5 Soi Raewadee 14,
Tanon Tiwanon,
Tambol Talad Kwan, Nontaburi
11000, Thailand
shii@loxinfo.co.th
Vithaya Pansringarm (President)

AUSTRALIA
Australian Kendo Renmei Incorporated
PO Box 353,
North Carlton, Victoria, 3054,
Australia
secretary@kendoaustralia.asn.au
www.kendoaustralia.asn.au
Ron Bennett (President)

NEW ZEALAND
New Zealand Kendo Federation
82a Bay Rd., St Heliers, Auckland,
New Zealand
Graham Sayer (President)
gandc@xtra.co.nz

UNITED KINGDOM
The British Kendo Association
31 Woodstock Rise, Sutton, Surrey,
GB-SM3 9JE, United Kingdom
howell.kendo@virgin.net
www.kendo.org.uk
John E Howell (Chairman)

EUROPE
European Kendo Federation (EKF)
c/o R Bernaers, Secretary General,
Lepelstraat 26, B-9140 TEMSE
(Steendorp), Belgium
secretary@ekf-eu.com
www.ekf-eu.com/
Alain Ducarme (President)
ANDORRA
Associacio Andorrana de Kendo
Ed. El Noguer 1, 3-4, Urb. La Clota,
Ordino Principat d'Andorra
aaken@elite-group.org
Miquel Morancho (President)

AUSTRIA

Austrian Kendo Association
Markfeldgasse 4/5, A-2380,
Perchtoldsdorf, Austria
d.hauck@netway.at
http://kendo.nwy.at
Dieter Hauck (President)

BELGIUM

All Belgium Kendo Federation
c/o Daniel Delepiere,
Bosbessenlaan 6, B-1930, Overijse,
Belgium
president@abkf.be
www.abkf.be
Daniel Delepiere (President)

DENMARK

Danish Kendo Federation
c/o Jens Jensen, Skovvangsvej 58,
st. tv. 8200 Aarhus N, Denmark
dkf@kendo.dk
www.kendo.dk
Jens Jensen (President)

CZECH REPUBLIC

Czech Kendo Federation
c/o Tomas Jelen,
Vrsovicka 40,
101 00, Praha 10,
Czech Republic
kendo_ckf@lycos.com
http://kendo.euweb.cz
Miloslav Hotovec (President)

FINLAND

Finnish Kendo Association
Aininkuja 2, SF-28400 ULVILA,
Finland
www.kendoliitto.net
ari.lehtinen@nic.fi
Ari Lehtinen (President)

FRANCE

Comité National de Kendo/FFJDA
21-25 Avenue de la Porte de
Chatillon
75014 Paris, France
kendo@ffjudo.com
www.ffjda.com/Kendo/discipline11.htm
Jean Pierre Soulas (President)

GERMANY

Deutscher Kendobund (DKenB)
c/o R Jattkowski, Handelalee 29,
D-10557 Berlin, Germany
info@dkenb.de
www.dkenb.de
Rainer Jattkowski (President)

HUNGARY

Hungarian Kendo Federation
Ribary u, 12, H-1022, Budapest,
Hungary
office@kendo.hu
Zsolt Vadadi (President)

ICELAND

Icelandic Kendo Federation
Laugateigur 35, IS-105, Reykjavik,
Iceland
Tryggvi Sigurdsson (President)

IRELAND

Kendo na h-Eireann
Peter Sherriff, 17 Devonshire St.,
Cork City, Republic of Ireland
info@kendo-ireland.com
Peter Sherriff (President)

ITALY

Confederazione Italiana Kendo
c/o Ms D Castelli, CIK Vice President,
Via Firenze 7, I-20025, Legnano,
(MI), Italy
www.kendo-cik.it
Mauro Navilli (President)
presidente@kendo-cik.it

LUXEMBURG

Shobukai Kendo Luxembourg
B.P. 1258, L-1012, Luxembourg
n.hanck@internet.lu
www.shobukai.lu
Norbert Hanck (President)

NETHERLANDS

Nederlandse Kendo Renmei
Noten Bogerd 17,
3343 BG Hendrik-Ido-Ambacht,
Netherlands
www.nkr.nl
h.odinot@nkr.nl
Hein Odinot (President)

NORWAY

Norwegian Kendo Federation
PO Box 10, 5877 Bergen, Norway
Alu98kalun@stud.hib.no
hikimen2002@yahoo.no
Magnus.rygh@objectware.no
kp@urbanarchitects.net
Kare Jon Lund (President)

POLAND

Polska Komisja Kendo
Saperow 1a, PL-94-316,
Lodz, Poland
c/o Secretary General,
Dereniowa 9 m 21, PL-02-776,
Warszawa, Poland
kendo@kendo.pl
www.kendo.pl

PORTUGAL

Associação Portuguesa de Kendo
c/o S Andrade,
Rua dr Rafael Duque 6-7 dr,
P-1500-250, Lisboa, Portugal
sergio@cnpd.pt
www.kendo.pt./kendo.htm
Sergio Andrade (President)

ROMANIA

Romanian Kendo Association

CP 121, OP 22, Bucharest,

Sector 1, Romania

gnelu@hotmail.com,

eugen.dumitrescu@ravantivirus.com

http://kendo.home.ro

Ion Garbea (President)

RUSSIA

Russian Kendo Federation

Proezd Kadomtseva, d. 17,

kv.55, RU-129128, Moscow, Russia

aloev@orgkendo.ru

aloevkendo@yahoo.com

www.orgkendo.ru

Rouslan Aloev (President)

SPAIN

Real Federacion Espanola de Judo y

Deportes Asociados

C/Ferraz, 16,7 Izqda, E-28008,

Madrid, Spain

Alejandro Blanco Bravo (President)

Emilio Serna (Vice President, Kendo)

SWEDEN

Swedish Budo & Martial Arts

Federation

Idrottens Hus Se-123 87,

Farsta, Sweden

kendo@budokampsport.se

www.budokampsport.se/kendo

Leif Sunje (President)

Mari Bacquin (Kendo Board)

SWITZERLAND

Swiss Kendo and Iaido, SJV/FSJ

Postfach 6905, CH-3001 Bern,

Switzerland

info@kendo.ch

www.kendo.ch

Ryuji Itoh (President)

YUGOSLAVIA

Yugoslav Kendo Federation

Bul. Mihajla Pupina 10d / II lokal br. 5,

N.Beograd 11070, Yugoslavia

wolf@ptt.yu (EKF/IKF Rep.)

www.kendo_serbia

Nikola Arbutina (President)

Vladan Vukic (EKF/IKF Rep.)

NORTH AMERICA

CANADA

Canadian Kendo Federation

205 Riviera Dr.,

Unit No.1, Markham,

Ontario L3R 5J8, Canada

rtasa@kendo-canada.com

http://kendo-canada.com/

Roy Asa (President)

MEXICO

Mexican Kendo Federation

Tenayuca 37-4, Col. Vertiz Narvarte,

C.P. 03600, Mexico, D.F.

adalberto_chavez@hotmail.com

Adalberto Chavez (President)

UNITED STATES OF AMERICA

All United States Kendo Federation

1156 Blackfield Dr.,

Santa Clara, CA

USA 95051

ktanaka1115@aol.com

www.auskf.info

Charlie Tanaka (President)

Hawaii Kendo Federation

2115 Brown Way, Honolulu, HI

USA 96822-1973

Terushi Ueno (President)

terter@Hawaii.rr.com

Dick Teshima (Vice President)

www.hawaiikendo.com

SOUTH AMERICA

ARGENTINA

Federacion Argentina de Kendo

San Martin 1420 (3400)

Corrientes,

Republica Argentina

estudiojuridicopm@impsat1.com.ar

fscaramellini@infovia.com.ar

Pedro Zacarias (President)

ARUBA

Kendo Aruba/Bun Bu Ichi

Mazurka 13, Cunucu Abao, Aruba

(Dutch Caribbean)

Kendoaru@setarnet.aw

Sergio A Velasquez (Chairman)

BRAZIL

All Brazil Kendo Federation

Rua Valerio de Carvalho,

63, Pinheiros,

Sao Paulo, Brazil,

CEP 05422 040

Tadachi Tamaki (President)

CHILE

Chilean Kendo Federation

Paris 748 of. 65 Santiago de Chile,

Chile

kendochile@entelchile.net

Jose Antonio Lanio (President)

VENEZUELA

Federacion Venezolana de Kendo

Ave. Sucre Dos Caminos,

8va. Transv.,

Cruce con Ave. Avila,

Qta. Lourdes, Caracas 071,

Venezuela

Hector Fuenmayor (President)

shonenbendo@hotmail.com

arielpintos@cantv.net

www.kenzendojo.s5.dom

GLOSSARY AND PRONUNCIATION GUIDE

Pronunciation guide

a is pronounced as in f**a**ther

e is pronounced as in m**e**t

i is pronounced as in b**i**kini

o is pronounced as in h**o**pe

u is pronounced as in fl**u**te

Combined vowels retain their individual sound, and each takes up one syllable. E.g., the word 'maai' is a three-syllable word, 'ma-a-i'.

Consonants are similar to English with the exception of **g**, which is always hard, as in '**g**et.'

Kendo terminology

Aiuchi — simultaneous strikes by both kendoka that cancel each other out

Ashi — the foot (also the leg)

Ashi sabaki — footwork

Ayumi ashi — walking where the feet cross on each step

Bassoku — penalty

Bogu — kendo armour

Bokuto (bokken) — wooden sword used for practising *kata*

Bushi — a member of the warrior class of feudal Japan

Chudan no kamae — the middle stance; tip points at the opponent's throat

Chui — caution; a match warning

Dan — a level or grade in kendo

Datotsu-bu — the section of the *shinai* which must be used for striking; the section from the *nakayui* forward

Debana waza — seizing the initiative and striking just as the opponent begins to move to attack

Do — the side of the torso; also, the piece of kendo armour which protects the abdomen and chest

Dogi — the uniform in kendo

Dojo — 'the place of the way,' a training hall.

Encho — overtime, to decide a match when no points have been scored

Fumikomi ashi — the foot which stamps as the strike is executed

Gedan no kamae — low level stance; sword tip points at the ground

Gogi — referees' discussion

Gokaku geiko — practice between kendoka of roughly equal skill

Hajime — 'Begin!' (start a match)

Hakama — pleated split-skirt worn in kendo and other martial arts; also worn at formal occasions in Japan

Hanshi — a master teacher, the highest honorary title awarded

Hantei — decision; judgement

Hansoku — a foul; referee's call

Hara — the belly

Harai waza — creating an opening in the opponent's stance by sweeping his *shinai* aside, and then attacking

Hasso no kamae — the mid-upper stance; sword held on the right, with the hand guard near the mouth and the blade angled slightly back

Hayasuburi — jumping forward and backward, cutting with each forward movement

Hidari — left, the left side

Hiki waza — stepping-back technique

Hikiwake — a draw

Iaido — the associated sword art of drawing and cutting with a real sword

Issoku itto no maai — 'one step, one sword distance' — either kendoka can strike by taking one step forward

Jodan no kamae — the upper level stance; the sword is held overhead, angled up

Kaeshi waza — techniques to block an attack, and immediately flip the sword, using some of the momentum from the attack to counterattack

Kakari geiko — all-out attacking

Kamae — a stance; often referring to *chudan no kamae*

Kata — a set form, or predetermined series of movements to practise attack and defence with a partner

Katana — Japanese sword

Keikogi — the jacket part of the kendo uniform

Kendo — the way of the sword

Kendo-gu — kendo equipment

Kendoka — one who practises kendo

Kenjutsu — 'the art of the sword', an earlier form of sword practice, out of which kendo was formed

Kiai — a shout used to channel and demonstrate one's spirit

Ki Ken Tai Ichi — 'Spirit Sword Body as One'; in practice, a simultaneous *kiai*, strike, and foot stamp; coordination of body, sword and intellect

Kirikaeshi — 'continuous cutting' exercise

Kote — forearm (also protective glove)

Kyoshi — teacher of seventh dan or higher

Kyu — a beginner's grade

Maai — dynamic combination of timing and distance between combatants

Men — the helmet; head

Migi — right, the right side

Mokuso — a period of meditation before and after kendo practice

Monomi — the gap between the bars of the *men*, through which one looks

Monouchi — the cutting portion of the sword blade; forward ⅓ of the blade

Motodachi — receiver of a technique; also the one who takes the role of instructor

Nidan waza — two-step techniques

Nihonto — Japanese sword

Nuki waza — moving the target out of the opponent's range, then striking at the opening created

Oji waza — techniques used to respond to an opponent's attack (counterattack)

Okuri ashi — leading foot is moved first in the direction of travel, and the trailing foot moved up to follow

Rei — a bow

Renshi — instructor, sixth *dan* and higher

Ritsu-rei — a standing bow

Ryuha — a traditional school or style of a particular art

Sageto — standing with the *shinai* hanging in the left hand

Sayu-men — the upper right and left corners of the head; strikes to these areas

Seiza — sitting on one's heels

Seme — forward pressure exerted with the *shinai*

Shibori — wringing of the hands, done at the instant of impact to tighten the grip on the *shinai*

Shidachi — in paired practice, the person who responds to uchidachi's movements with counterattacks

Shikake-waza — creating an opening in an opponent's stance, and attacking

Shinai — a practice sword used in kendo, made up of the following components:

    chigiri — a metal square used as a spacer in the *shinai* handle

    datotsu-bu — the section of the *shinai* from the *nakayui* forward; the valid striking section of the *shinai*

    kensen — tip of the *shinai* or sword

    nakayui — strip of leather wound around the *shinai* at the forward ⅓, delineating the *datotsu-bu* and holding the staves together

    saki-gawa — the leather cap at the tip of the *shinai*

    shin — T-shaped rubber stopper at the tip of the *shinai*, inside the *sakigawa* and between the ends of the bamboo staves (also *sakigomi*)

    take — the bamboo staves

    tsuka — the handle of the *shinai*

    tsuka-gashira — end of the *tsuka*

    tsuka-gawa — the leather cover over the *tsuka*

    tsuba — the round hand guard, made of hard leather or plastic

    tsubadome — rubber stopper which holds the *tsuba* in place

    tsuru — the string that connects the leather portions of the *shinai* (*sakigawa, nakayui, tsuka-gawa*) and holds the *shinai* together

Shinpan — a referee

Shinpancho — the chief referee

Shinsa — a grading

Shinzen — small shrine inside a *dojo*

Shobu-ari — a judge's call meaning 'there is a winner'

Shomen — the top, centre of the head; also the focal point of a *dojo* that does not have a shrine

Sonkyo — the deep squat assumed before and after a match

Suigetsu — point in the centre of the body below the ribcage; solar plexus

Suriashi — sliding footwork

Tai-atari — a body check

Taito — position assumed when the *shinai* is held against the left hip

Tanden — a point two inches below the navel, thought to be the centre of breathing and energy

Tare — apron-like waist protector

Tenugui — rectangular piece of cloth, often with printed Japanese calligraphy, worn on the head under the *men*, to absorb sweat

Torikeshi — cancellation of a point

Tsubazeriai — position where kendoka clash with hands at waist level

Tsuki — a thrust to the throat

Uchidachi — initiates the movements in a *kata* and controls the combative distance by choosing when to attack

Uwagi — jacket (also *keiko-gi*)

Waki-gamae — the sword is held behind the body, with hands at the right hip

Waza — technique

Yame — the command to stop

Zanshin — 'the heart that lingers,' continued awareness after an attack

Zekken — a name tag, worn over the centre flap of the *tare*

INDEX

PHOTOGRAPHIC CREDITS

2,   Kenneth Hamm/Photo Japan

4—5 Kenneth Hamm/Photo Japan

9   Mark Hemmings/Photo Japan

12   Bridgeman Art Library/ The Stapleton Collection

13   Maidstone Museum and Art Gallery/ Bridgeman Art Library

15   Istituto Geografico De Agostini

16   Mark Hemmings/Photo Japan

17   Mark Hemmings/Photo Japan

22   Bethnal Green Museum/Bridgeman Art Library

29   Mark Hemmings/Photo Japan

37   New Holland Image Library/Nicholas Aldridge

54   Istituto Geografico De Agostini

78   Gallo Images / gettyimages.com—